MW00328874

Texas Old-Time Restaurants and Cafes

Sheryl Smith-Rodgers

Republic of Texas Press

HOUSTON PUBLIC LIBRARY

. R01153 79671

Library of Congress Cataloging-in-Publication Data

Smith-Rodgers, Sheryl.
  Texas old-time restaurants and cafes / Sheryl Smith-Rodgers.
     p. cm.
  Includes index.
  ISBN 1-55622-733-7 (pbk.)
  1. Roadside restaurants--Texas. 2. Cookery--Texas. I. Title.

TX945.S573   2000
647.95764--dc21

00-024564
CIP

© 2000, Sheryl Smith-Rodgers

All Rights Reserved

Republic of Texas Press is an imprint of Wordware Publishing, Inc.

No part of this book may be reproduced in any form or by
any means without permission in writing from
Wordware Publishing, Inc.

Printed in the United States of America

ISBN 1-55622-733-7
10 9 8 7 6 5 4 3 2 1
0006

All inquiries for volume purchases of this book should be addressed to
Wordware Publishing, Inc., at 2320 Los Rios Boulevard, Plano, Texas
75074. Telephone inquiries may be made by calling:

(972) 423-0090

For the best parents
in the world.

Mine.

Harry and Marcelle Smith.

You always encouraged me.
Thank you.
I love you.

Contents

To the north

Contents

And one you've never heard of . . .

Foreword

Restaurants hold a special place in our memory. Like the chapters of a novel, they tell the story of our lives. Unfortunately, many of the restaurants where we spent endless hours as teenagers, celebrated special occasions, or launched new business ventures are like fading memories, crowded out of existence in today's fast paced world.

This book is a tribute to those restaurateurs who have had the skill and tenacity to command loyalty from consumers who are ever tempted by a host of new dining opportunities. Twenty-plus years of business in an industry where one-third of all new restaurants fail in the first year is a remarkable feat.

I hope that you not only have an opportunity to enjoy the recipes selected for this publication, but that you have the occasion to enjoy the restaurants highlighted in these pages. There is always another memory waiting to be made in that special restaurant where we celebrate life's joys.

Richie Jackson
Executive vice president/CEO
Texas Restaurant Association
Austin, Texas

Introduction

Have a seat an' make ya'self at home!

Small-town cafes. Big-city restaurants. Texas claims thousands of them. More than 60,000, to be precise. If you're a native Texan, you probably have some favorites. And more than likely, they're the ones you remember from way back, places that you frequented with your grandparents during the summer or where you ate a meal while on the road with your parents at Christmas. Amazingly, hundreds of those same restaurants are still around these many years later. Some boast lots of atmosphere and a few gimmicks, like the Big Texan Steak Ranch in Amarillo. Still others are more refined and elegant, such as the Green Pastures Restaurant in Austin and the Grey Moss Inn near Helotes. Many double as a community watering hole, where the locals gather to drink coffee and discuss what's happening around town. The Bowling Alley Cafe in Blanco (my town) and the Blue Bonnet in Marble Falls fit that bill.

Large or small, fancy or plain, these restaurants share three things in common—long histories, established reputations, and loyal customers. Lots of the latter. Or else I figure they wouldn't still be in business after twenty-plus years and claim all those colorful histories.

If you're not a native Texan, then allow one to introduce you to a collection of our state's tried-and-true dining establishments. I'll be honest and admit that I didn't visit every one during the course of writing this book. But I've eaten at many during my forty-odd years of living in Texas, so I can claim past experience at least. Neither does *Texas Old-Time Restaurants* claim to name the best of 'em or even ALL of them. That would be next to impossible. Instead, I gathered the names of places I knew had been around a long while, visited as many as I could, and implored the owners of others to fill me in on their special restaurant. My list of "old" restaurants and cafes numbered more than a hundred. And I know Texas has far, far more than that.

How did I find these restaurants? All kinds of ways. First, as I mentioned, I knew about many of them myself, like Barth's in Kenedy, Frank's Spaghetti House in Corpus Christi, the Bon Ton in La Grange, and the O.S.T. in Bandera. Friends, other restaurant owners, and staff at chambers of commerce suggested more. My pal and fellow author Larry D. Hodge of Marble Falls often emailed me with restaurant names while on the road gathering research for his own books (I'll name one . . . *Good Times in Texas: A Pretty Complete Guide to Where the Fun Is*, Republic of Texas Press). What's more, he photographed several restaurants for me, which you'll see on the following pages (I owe him . . . just what, I don't know, but Larry will come up with something, I'm sure).

When I could find them, I scoured guidebooks on Texas cafes and jotted down names of potential candidates for my book. Then I got on the Internet, and using the Yellow Pages through Yahoo.com, I looked to see if they were still in business. If they were, I copied the addresses and phone numbers. Then I called the restaurants.

Once, I took a chance and emailed a newspaper columnist out of the blue. Bill Whitaker with the *Abilene Reporter-News* promptly wrote me back and suggested the Dixie Pig Restaurant, which opened in 1931. Voila! Another cafe to add to my list! (Thanks, Bill.)

How did restaurants qualify for my list? I looked for ones that were twenty or more years old (the older, the better) and had kept the same name all those years. If a restaurant moved or changed owners, that was OK. I do have some exceptions, like the Black Bear Restaurant at Davis Mountains State Park and a few others. I threw in a couple of old drug stores because many of us recall eating burgers and slurping malts at the soda fountain. Sadly, many of them are long gone now. As for old barbecue joints, I only included one and let fellow author Richard K. Troxell of Fredericksburg introduce those to you in his recent book *Barbecuing Around Texas* (Republic of Texas Press). All in all, though, *Texas Old-time Restaurants* pays tribute to a group of venerable cafes that have withstood the test of time and kept the customers coming.

As a fun aside, I also learned during my research for this book that many Texas restaurants share the same name or similar variations. For instance, the Bluebonnet Cafe in Temple is named for our state flower, the bluebonnet. The Blue Bonnet Cafe in Marble Falls, though, is named for a woman's hat. Several restaurants go by the simple name of City Cafe, such as those in Sterling City and Elgin. And did you know that at least three restaurants share a barnyard animal in common? The Pig Stand in Beaumont, the Dixie Pig Restaurant in Abilene, and the Juicy Pig Cafe in Sherman. The first Pig Stand opened in 1921 in Dallas. The Dixie Pig followed in '31, and then the Juicy Pig opened in '36.

Speaking of animal names, would you believe there's one place called the Green Frog Restaurant in Jacksboro?

As for the recipes, I didn't make those mandatory. Many restaurant owners gladly submitted a few when I asked. John and Belinda Kemper at the Blue Bonnet in Marble Falls generously sent me a copy of their cookbook, *What's Cooking at the Blue Bonnet Cafe*, and said I could pick out what I wanted to include. So did Bud Royers at Royers' Round Top Cafe in Round Top and Brenda Mitchell at the Wunsche Bros. Cafe & Saloon in Spring. Bennie Martin at Martin's Restaurant in Lampasas showed me the kitchen's collection of recipes typed decades ago on large index cards, all stained and yellowed with use. Don Wise at Andy's Diner in Fredericksburg kindly jotted down two potato recipes, as did a number of others. A few folks emailed theirs to me. Where recipes are lacking, likely the restaurant's policy prohibited sharing any or cooks there prepare dishes by memory.

Memories . . . I shared a few of mine along the way in this book. I hope you don't mind. After all, the pages of our pasts, the many happy and sad, fun and frustrating times, make us who we are today. The cafes and restaurants where we ate as children and shared conversation with our parents are part of those chapters. When we discover as adults that those places still exist, still even look the same, we find a comfort and special connection to our past that's hard to explain. We only know we feel good being there again. For instance, go back to Barth's, as I did for this book, and you'll see a white lollipop tree still standing near the front door, the very same one I remember from my childhood. It *is* comforting to know that a few simple things in life haven't changed after all.

So go back to your roots or see some new country. Along the way, you're bound to pass some tried-and-true, old-time Texas restaurants. Pull off the road, step inside, and claim a seat. You're in for a treat. Or else, as I figure, that place would not still be around after all these years.

Sheryl Smith-Rodgers

To the north

Amarillo

Big Texan Steak Ranch
(1960)

Another Panhandle evening descends upon the Big Texan Steak Ranch in Amarillo, and a "horse guy," perched high in the saddle, greets delighted guests in the restaurant's parking lot.

"Yeah, I park cars," drawls the cowboy-style valet as his horse stamps a foot impatiently. "But I also take people for rides, young and old."

Go ahead. Climb aboard and go for a quick jaunt around the parking lot with the horse guy. Then step inside the western-style restaurant and loosen up your belt because a meal at the Big Texan is no ordinary dining experience. Here you may see a customer attempt to down a monstrous 72-ounce steak or a scruffy mountain man start a small fire right at your table. Throughout the evening, you'll be serenaded by roaming guitarists belting out such familiar Texas tunes as "Deep in the Heart of Texas" and "Orange Blossom Special."

R.J. Lee opened the Big Texan in 1960 after he discovered Amarillo lacked a real Texas-style steak house. The diner quickly gained popularity, largely due to its famous 72-ounce steak. Anyone downing the platter-sized slab of meat and side dishes (baked potato, salad, shrimp cocktail, and a roll) within an hour, Lee promised, would get the meal free.

Lee has since died, but three of his sons—Danny, Doug, and Bobby—continue the restaurant's world-famous tradition. In fact, more than 27,000 beef-lovers have accepted the Big Texan challenge (that's a lot of bull, brags the over-sized menu), and more than 4,500 have licked their plates clean within the allotted time. A chalkboard near the front door lists the names and comments of recent meat-guzzling champs. "What's for dessert?" scrawled Sam McCarty, a Floridian who consumed his meal just one second shy of an hour. Among the best-remembered finishers are Cincinnati Reds pitcher Frank Pastoria (he gulped his feast down in 9.5 minutes in 1983), an 11-year-old boy, and a spry 63-year-old grandmother.

"We want everyone to win here," Danny Lee says. "They're not going to brag if they lose."

Gaudy and showy, the huge dining room resembles the movie set of a shoot-'em-up Western, complete with wooden tables, wagon wheel chandeliers, and an old-fashioned stove bearing an ample pan of corn bread and a big pot of the day's soup. At any moment, you might almost expect a bad guy to topple down from the encircling second-floor balcony, trimmed with a wooden balustrade and adorned with an abundance of mounted animal heads, such as mule deer, aoudads, and even a moose.

Not up to a 72-ounce steak? The Big Texan dishes up plenty of other menu choices. Less hungry appetites can choose from steak dinners (big and small), salads, sandwiches, chicken-fried steak, chicken, and even fried shrimp. An "over 55" menu section caters to seniors, and all kids' meals come with a free cowboy hat. Find a partner or two, then order the strawberry shortcake. "It's so big, we give non-Texans three forks," the menu proclaims.

When you're done dining, mosey over to the arcade, filled with games and a shooting gallery. Stock up on Texas souvenirs in the gift shop, and then take a gander at the "Den of Death," a huge glass case containing a 6-foot, 8-pound diamondback rattlesnake.

Visit the restaurant on a Tuesday, and you'll be treated to Big Texan Opry, a foot-stomping evening of music and clogging. Reservations are recommended but not required. Stay the night if you like at Big Texan's motel, built to resemble a Western frontier town. There's even a Texas-shaped swimming pool.

Gettin' there: On eastern edge of Amarillo, located between the Whitaker and Lakeside exits on Interstate 40.

Big Texan Steak Ranch
7701 I-40 East
Amarillo, TX 79118
806/372-6000
800/657-7177
Website: www.amaonline.com/bigtexan

Stop by and see: The infamous Cadillac Ranch is a "crop" of ten Cadillacs (circa 1948 to 1963) originally planted nose down in 1974 by Amarillo businessman and philanthropist Stanley Marsh III. This unforgettable sight is buried in a field 9 miles west of town on I-40. Even more awesome and breathtaking sights lie 25 miles south of Amarillo at Palo Duro State Park, which preserves the country's second largest canyon. Vistas there are absolutely stunning.

Big Texan Texas Caviar

2 cans (16-oz. each) black-eyed peas, drained
1 medium jalapeño, minced
$\frac{1}{4}$ small white onion, chopped
$\frac{1}{3}$ cup Italian dressing
$\frac{1}{2}$ green bell pepper, chopped

1 teaspoon seasoned salt
2 teaspoons chili powder
2 teaspoons ground cumin
$\frac{1}{4}$ teaspoon ground red pepper

Combine black-eyed peas with remaining ingredients. Serve chilled with corn chips. Makes 5 cups.

Golden Light Cafe
(1946)

Walk along Sixth Street along old Route 66, and you might just pass the Golden Light without even noticing it. That's because from the outside, the red-bricked cafe looks rather plain. Maybe even a little bit . . . well . . . seedy. Iron bars grip the windows, and a lone park bench sits outside the white door. Stop and read the posted menus, though, and you'll learn that the Golden Light—Amarillo's oldest eatery and the oldest restaurant on Route 66 in continuous operation—has quite a respectful history. It's even listed in the National Register of Historic Places.

Chester "Pop" Ray and his wife, Louise, started the business in 1946. A week before it was set to open, Pop got sick. So his son and daughter-in-law, Charles and Edye, agreed to take over. Charles grabbed some plywood and hurriedly built a few booths. Between the two of them, they flipped burgers, waited tables, and grossed $10.48 the first day. Pop recovered a few weeks later and ran the cafe until 1957. He sold the restaurant and died 14 years later at the age of 82. A few more owners have come and gone through the years. Marc Reed has run the place since 1990, when he bought it at the age of 21.

"The decor at the Golden Light hasn't changed much since '46, except for the addition of a beer garden in the back," says Linda Reed, his mother. "Marc still has some of the same customers that Pop had back then. Nowadays, the crowd here is very eclectic. On any day, you'll see businessmen in coats and ties, cowboys in boots and jeans, and Harley riders in black leather."

Marc serves pretty much the same grub as Pop did—burgers and a few sandwiches. He added his own inventions, too, like Flagstaff Pie (Frito pie), Half Way to Albuquerque (a giant chile burrito), All the Way to LA (a chile burrito with special toppings), and Marc's Sixth Street Special (recipe follows). He also cooks up specials, like quesadillas, fajitas, and salads.

Besides burgers, Pop used to make a mean pot of chili. Subsequent owners developed their own recipes, which they politely declined to share with Marc. So he developed his own, a concoction he calls Route 66 Chili. "Don't even think about asking for it," he warns on the menu.

Gettin' there: From I-40, exit on Georgia Street. Head north on Georgia to Sixth Street; turn left on Sixth. The Golden Light is approximately two blocks down on the right.

Golden Light Cafe
2908 W. Sixth Ave.
Amarillo, TX 79106
806/374-9237

Stop by and see: In Amarillo, look out for some of the most unusual road signs you'll ever see. Shaped like highway department road signs, the quirky metal signs, painted with pictures and/or strange phrases, can be spotted in parking lots, back alleys, residential yards, in front of businesses, and along roadsides. Created and painted by local artists, the signs are funded by the (in)famous Stanley Marsh III.

Marc's Sixth Street Special
$\frac{1}{4}$-pound hamburger patty
1 slice American or cheddar cheese
$\frac{1}{2}$ cup chopped tomato
$\frac{1}{4}$ cup sour cream
dash hot sauce
1 large flour tortilla

Season hamburger with salt and pepper; cook on grill. Top meat with cheese during the last few minutes of cooking. Place meat, cheese, chopped tomato, sour cream, and hot sauce on heated tortilla. Serve while hot.

Arlington

Al's Hamburgers
(1957)

You can't keep a good man down for long. That especially holds true for Al Mathews. He's has been knocked down a few times, but each time he's come back stronger. Otherwise, his Arlington institution, Al's Hamburgers, wouldn't have survived for more than four decades.

Al and his wife, Thelma, got into the hamburger business in Dallas in 1949. For seven years, they ran a Freez Ette franchise that sold soft-serve ice cream and hot dogs. In 1957 the couple opened a burger stand in north Arlington, then a rural community. Many a morning Al had to chase cows out of the parking lot before he could open his drive-in. As the area developed, Al's Hamburgers became more popular. The cows disappeared, too. Ironically, the town's thriving growth, once a boon for Al's business, later caused the restaurant's temporary demise. Seeing the rise in real estate values, the owner of the property where Al's Hamburgers was located decided to sell the tract in 1986. In the name of profit and progress, Al's Hamburgers would be razed to make way for a modern strip shopping center.

Wanting to go out in style, the Mathews in April 1986 rented a big tent, set it up in an adjoining field, and hosted a huge farewell party. Droves of people attended. By midnight, only 83 buns of the 4,000 ordered were left. With the restaurant closed, Al and Thelma looked forward to a year of leisure and travel. After that, they'd find a new location and reopen the restaurant.

Sadly, their plans went awry six months later when Al woke up one morning partially paralyzed. His diagnosis: Guillain-Barre Syndrome, a rare illness that affects the peripheral nerves of the body. He spent seven weeks in a hospital. Finally, after months of daily rehabilitation, Al once again walked unaided.

As they say, you can't keep a good man down. Or a great restaurant. In 1989 Al and Thelma along with their daughter, Melody, reopened Al's Hamburgers in the corner of—ironically—a strip center in Arlington. Many of the original staff returned and so did the customers. In droves.

Like he always has, Al, wearing his trademark white apron, cooks his burgers on an old, well-seasoned grill. The buns toast right next to them. In the final stages of cooking, Al carefully places the buns on top of the patties so they absorb the meat's fragrant steam. One of his best sellers is the chili-cheese burger topped with bacon. Customers with big appetites like to order the triple hamburgers (THREE patties!) and cheeseburgers (three patties AND three slices of cheese!!). The menu also touts a few salads, "non-burgers" (grilled chicken sandwiches, ham and cheese, BLTs, turkey clubs, and steak sandwiches), "plates and such" (chicken-fried steak, grilled chicken, catfish, fried shrimp, and Frito pie), French fries, onion rings, tater tots, pie, and cheesecake.

Gettin' there: Al's is located at the corner of North Collins Street and Green Oaks Boulevard in Arlington.

Al's Hamburgers
1001 NE Green Oaks Blvd.

Arlington, TX 76016
817/275-8918

Stop by and see: The Legends of the Game Baseball Museum
and Learning Center at the Ballpark in Arlington showcases
hundreds of baseball memorabilia plus lots of interactive
exhibits.

Al's Chili-Cheese Burger with Bacon

one fresh-ground chuck patty
American cheese
good chili
chopped onions
mustard
fried bacon
one hamburger bun

Separate and toast bun on griddle. Fry meat patty until done
but not dry. Place cheese and bacon on top of patty; place
top bun on top of patty. Spread mustard on bottom bun;
add onions and chili. Place top bun over bottom and serve.
Very tasty!

Mexican Salad

Cover the bottom of a dinner platter with Fritos; crush. Add
lettuce and onions. Ring the platter with chopped fresh
tomatoes. Place a small mound of picante sauce in the middle of the salad. Pour ladle of chili over the top. Sprinkle
with grated cheddar cheese. Serve!

Arlington Steak House
(1931)

The Arlington Steak House opened in 1931 as the Triangle Inn,
a barbecue joint on Division Street.

"It wasn't even in the city of Arlington back then," tells
present owner Chris Odell. "As the town grew, it grew around
the restaurant."

Chris isn't sure who originally built the business, which was changed to the Arlington Steak House in the late forties. Through the years, the menu has evolved to include Mexican food and seafood plates. Pit barbecue is still served, and steaks are popular with customers. But the top seller is the steak house's chicken-fried steaks. "We were voted 'best chicken-fried steak in Arlington' by the *Arlington Star-Telegram*," Odell says. "We're also famous for our hot yeast rolls. We bake them twice a day."

In the late thirties, the restaurant was also famous for another reason. Or maybe we should say INfamous. . . . "There was illegal gambling here at one time on the second floor," Odell shares. "It was supposed to be a secret, but everyone knew about it."

Gettin' there: From the east, take I-30 West; head south on State Highway 360; take Division Street exit; turn right and head west on Division. Arlington Steak House will be on the left a couple of miles down, past Fielder Road.

Arlington Steak House
1724 W. Division St.
Arlington, TX 76012
817/275-7881

Candlelite Inn
(1957)

Chris Odell owns another old Arlington institution on Division Street. It's called the Candlelite Inn. The Keith family originally opened the business in 1957 as a small drive-in. Later, they built a larger facility behind the original drive-in and renamed it. Odell bought the restaurant in 1992 from the Keiths.

"As far as I can tell, it still has the same menu it had back then," he says, referring to the restaurant's eclectic mixture of food—pizza, steaks, spaghetti, burritos, tacos, salads, and burgers. "The inn was the first restaurant in Arlington to serve pizza," he adds.

By the way, here's a free history lesson: The reason so many old restaurants and motels are along Division Street is because Division once upon a time was the main east-to-west thorough-fare that connected Fort Worth, Arlington, and Dallas.

Gettin' there: From the east, take I-30 West; head south on State Highway 360; take Division Street exit; turn right and head west on Division. Candelite Inn will be on the left, after crossing Stadium Drive, but before Collins Street.

Candlelite Inn
1202 E. Division St.
Arlington, TX 76011
817/275-9613

Dallas

Celebration Restaurant
(1971)

"That hippie place that grows their own vegetables"—that's what folks used to call Celebration Restaurant soon after it opened. Seems the young men who ran the business had long hair, and back then long hair on a guy had to mean he was a hippie. Well, to set the record straight, they WERE hippies, but not hippies who grew veggies. They did, however, cook up lots and lots of fresh ones. And that's one of the big reasons Celebration Restaurant customers have kept coming back for nearly thirty years.

Started as Celebration Restaurant and Leather Shop, the business opened in a small house in 1971. Only dinner was served, and tables filled up quickly every night. While custom-ers waited for a seat, they could browse through the leather shop. Year by year, Celebration's base of patrons grew. Two more houses were added to the original one, and the leather shop was moved to another location to make room for a court-yard with a full-service bar. Lunch hours were also added. Eventually, the leather shop closed so owners could focus exclusively on the restaurant. In 1987 a second Celebration opened in Fort Worth.

Another feature folks love about Celebration's is the unusual "reorder" policy at dinner. Customers who order from the "traditional entrees" selection may ask for seconds on their entree or any entree of equal or less value. For example, order pot roast, and you'll get three vegetables (served family-style) along with your choice of soup, salad, or fresh fruit. THEN—if you have room—you can try the fried catfish, chicken-fried steak, meat loaf, baked chicken, chicken-fried chicken, or spa-ghetti. Nightly dinner specials often feature Jamaican jerk chicken, country-style pork ribs, Dijon chicken, and fried chicken. Celebration's is also known for wonderful pies, cob-blers, and banana pudding.

For lunch, you can choose from daily specials in addition to salads, sandwiches, soups, plate meals, and those beloved fresh, cooked vegetables . . . steamed new potatoes, black-eyed peas, glazed carrots, mashed potatoes, steamed cabbage, and steamed green beans.

Vegetables never had it so good.

Gettin' there: From the Dallas North Tollway southbound to the Northwest Highway (Loop 12) exit, turn right (west) onto Northwest Highway and continue to Inwood Road. Turn left (south) on Inwood and continue to Lovers Lane. Turn right (west) on Lovers Lane and continue about one mile. Celebra-tion will be on the right at the corner of Elsby.

Celebration Restaurant
4503 W. Lovers Lane
Dallas, TX 75209
214/358-0612

El Fenix Mexican Restaurant
(1918)

The Martinez family with the El Fenix Mexican Restaurant chain like to claim that they started the Tex-Mex food revolution. Well, actually it was their patriarch, Mike Martinez Sr., who took the first "shot," so to speak.

It all started in 1911 or so when Mike immigrated from Mexico to Dallas and went to work for the railroad. When he was laid off, he found a job washing dishes at a downtown hotel. After he'd worked his way up to chef's assistant, he decided to take the plunge and open his own place. In 1918 he opened El Fenix Cafe on McKinney Street, where the Woodall Rodgers Freeway now runs through downtown.

In the beginning, El Fenix stayed opened 'round the clock. During the days of World War II and meat rationing, though, the restaurant had to start closing. The story goes that since the business hadn't ever shut down, no one could find the key to the front door. So a locksmith had to make one. In the meantime, Mike and his family kept dishing up plates of enchiladas, tamales, beans, and rice.

According to the family history, the traditional Mexican "combination" plate started at the El Fenix. Back then, reputable restaurants served each dish on a separate plate. Mike did until, on evenings when he was the only hired hand in the kitchen, he decided he needed fewer dishes to wash. So he introduced the "combination" plate, which served everything—enchiladas, beans, and rice—on one platter.

When he opened his second El Fenix more than fifty years ago, Mike implemented a 95-cent "Wednesday enchilada special" as a marketing gimmick to attract new customers. The tradition, still in place (though priced substantially higher), has been borrowed by other Mexican restaurants.

Soon after his sons returned from WWII, Mike turned the business over to his eight children. He died in 1956. Today, the siblings and their children run the El Fenix chain, which includes sixteen locations in the Dallas area. They still serve their father's famous combination plate along with a large selection of other favorites—fajitas, chimichangas, flautas, steaks, tacos, grilled chicken, and more.

Gettin' there: El Fenix on McKinney Avenue is located at the corner of Field Street and McKinney in downtown Dallas near the West End. Take the Field Street exit off the Woodall Rodgers Freeway.

El Fenix Mexican Restaurant
1601 McKinney Ave.
Dallas, TX 75202
214/747-1121
Website: http://www.elfenixtexmex.com

Kuby's Sausage House
(1728-Germany, 1961-Dallas)

I first heard about Kuby's Sausage House from my good friend David Ries, who grew up near the popular restaurant and deli. "Dad and I used to eat there every time I returned home from school, and I still go there," he shares. "It's a wonderful place. Walk in, and you'll see old-fashioned sausage links hanging from the ceiling, pastries, German magazines, beer steins, and strudel!"

Kuby's goes back even further than my friend's childhood memories. WAY back. The original Kuby's meat market and restaurant opened in Kaiserslautern, Germany, in 1728. For fifteen generations, recipes, spice formulas, and sausage-making techniques were handed down from father to son, and the market stayed in business into the twentieth century. Then in 1956 Karl Kuby, the oldest son of Friedrich Kuby, immigrated from Germany to Texas. First he worked for an uncle in Harlingen. Then he moved to the Dallas area and worked at Rudolph's Meat Market. In 1961, at the age of 28, he opened his own market and restaurant in Snider Plaza and named it Kuby's Sausage House.

I got to visit Kuby's before I finished the manuscript for this book, compliments of Ginnie Bivona, an editor at Republic of Texas Press who recruited me for this project. Kuby's manager Elisabeth Williams, a native German, kindly talked with us about the business she's overseen since 1969.

"People have come here for years and years to buy the same things in the deli," she says, seated at a booth with us in the dimly lit dining room. "One man comes in, and I start slicing his meat as soon as I see him. Sometimes I get orders ready before the customers even come in."

What else do folks buy at Kuby's Sausage House, besides sausage? Oh, any number of things. The deli sells liverwurst, imported hams, smoked turkeys, beef, and smoked bacon, not to mention more than fifty varieties of sausage (all processed and smoked by Kuby staff). A display case offers the day's selection of salads, such as tuna fish, chicken, mustard potato, cucumber, and fresh sauerkraut. Another case stocks German-style breads, cookies, and pastries. Tall metal shelves in the market area display German jams, mustards, pickles, cereals, candy, and more. Kuby's also sells German magazines, German cosmetics, German chocolates, German greeting cards, and even German diaper rash cream.

In the adjoining restaurant, wooden stools at the long counter, booths along the walls, and numerous tables fill up fast at meal times. After ordering a German wiener with red cabbage and German potatoes, I absorbed the atmosphere and watched people come and go in the dining room. The wait staff, obviously long-time employees and well experienced, whisked back and forth between tables, taking orders and delivering plates laden with food. It wasn't long before our lunch arrived, and I bit into a crusty slice of fried potato. Wonderful. The wiener was pleasantly seasoned and the tangy red cabbage slightly crisp.

An especially lively time to visit Kuby's is a Friday or Saturday evening when accordion players entertain customers. But the truth is, anytime's a lively time at Kuby's. Just stop by sometime and see.

Gettin' there: From Central Expressway, go west on Mockingbird. Take a right on Hillcrest and a left on Daniel. Kuby's is straight ahead at 6601 Snider Plaza.

Kuby's Sausage House
6601 Snider Plaza
Dallas, TX 75205
214/363-2231

Mecca Restaurant
(1938)

Roy Redding and his two daughters, Frances and Patsy Redding, in 1938 opened the original Mecca Restaurant near Love Field. They kept the cafe open 'round the clock in the early years until they cut back when they decided some hours just weren't as profitable. To this day, the Mecca still serves only breakfast and lunch.

In the late eighties, Tom Schott and John Fooshee bought the business. "We still have some of the same employees who worked for Reddings," Tom says. They've kept the menu pretty much the same, too. Breakfast features eggs, omelettes, hot cakes, French toast, and cinnamon rolls. For lunch, you can order off the menu and choose from steaks, chicken, salads, and sandwiches. "Chicken-fried steak and chicken tenders are our best sellers," Tom says.

Or you can check out the weekly list of daily entrees and go from there. But beware—the number of choices is awesome. For instance, one Wednesday listed, as main entrees, chicken and dumplings, chicken-fried steak, grilled chicken breast, pork loin and dressing, hamburger steak, and fried catfish. THEN you have to figure out which side dishes you want: red beans, garden salad, whipped potatoes, corn bread dressing, creamed corn, spinach, scalloped potatoes, green beans, and carrots.

Lots of folks eat at the Mecca every day. "It's a good people-watching place," Tom says. "We have a lot of high-profile people from Dallas who come in to eat, from Cowboys to the mayor. You never know who you're going to see here."

Gettin' there: From I-35E N, take the Harry Hines Boulevard exit. Merge onto Raceway Drive. Turn left onto Harry Hines Boulevard. Mecca is one mile north of that intersection on the right-hand side of the street.

Mecca Restaurant
10422 Harry Hines Blvd.
Dallas, TX 75220
214/352-0051

Macaroni and Tomatoes

5 pounds macaroni
1 #10 can tomatoes (the BIG size)
1 pound margarine
3 tablespoons salt
2 tablespoons black pepper
water

Place tomatoes, salt, and pepper in a pot and bring to a boil. Place water in second stock pot and bring to a boil. Drop in pasta and cook until tender. Remove from heat and drain macaroni. Pour macaroni back in pot and add tomatoes and margarine. Stir well.

Denton
Texas Pickup Cafe
(1976)

And then there's the Texas Pickup Cafe, a long-time Denton tradition. Bill and Marion Graham in 1976 opened the cafe, which quickly became known as a "great hometown restaurant." Among its top-billed menu items were chicken-fried steak and French fries smothered in cheddar cheese. Out front still sits the Grahams' 1939 Ford pickup, the cafe's vintage mascot and local landmark.

Tony Worrell and Kenny Feigeles run the cafe these days. They changed the menu some but not the decor. They also kept the "license plate club" going, a tradition originally started when the cafe opened. Dozens of license plates line the walls, all signed by customers through the years. "This is a college town so we have a lot of people who leave, then come back years later to see the license plate they signed," Tony says. "People like to come in and see them. Grandparents come with their grandkids and show them the license plate they signed back in the seventies."

You can order just about anything at the Texas Pickup Cafe. The extensive menu includes lots of appetizers (like nachos, potato skins, quesadillas, chips with salsa, and stuffed jalapeños), salads, baked potatoes, hot and cold sandwiches, and burgers. "Hometown Dinners" feature chicken-fried steak, chicken tenders, barbecue chicken, lemon chicken, and Santa Fe chicken (covered with sauteed mushrooms, onions, and Swiss cheese). Vegetarians have their choice of a vegetable plate dinner, a veggie sandwich, and veggie soft tacos.

Gettin' there: The Pickup is located at the corner of West Prairie Street and Avenue E.

Texas Pickup Cafe
2101 W. Prairie St.
Denton, TX 76201
940/382-1221

Stop by and see: Evers Hardware Co., across from the county courthouse on the square, has been in operation since 1885. The original family still owns it, too.

This batter coats the Pickup's deep-fried mushrooms and onion rings.

20

Mushroom and Onion-Ring Batter

16 ounces cold beer
28 ounces flour
8 ounces buttermilk
2 ounces black pepper
2 ounces honey
2 ounces garlic powder
½ ounce salt

Stir and mix in one ingredient at a time.

The Pickup serves this tangy concoction as a dipping sauce. You'll also taste it on the Hickory Burger and Turkey Melt Sandwich.

Hickory Sauce

16 ounces barbecue sauce
16 ounces honey
3 ounces black pepper
6 ounces chili sauce

Stir and mix in one ingredient at a time.

Picante Sauce

1 gallon can crushed tomatoes
16 ounces jalapeños, chopped
16 ounces grilled onion, chopped
3 ounces black pepper
3 ounces garlic powder

Stir and mix in one ingredient at a time.

Wing Batter

16 ounces flour
4 ounces Lawry's seasoned salt
4 ounces cayenne powder
6 ounces buttermilk
3 ounces water

Stir and mix in one ingredient at a time.

Fort Worth

Angelo's
(1958)

For some great Texas barbecue, by George, stop by Angelo's in Fort Worth. Angelo George opened the popular eatery on St. Patrick's Day in 1958. His mainstays then—barbecue and beer served in frosty steins—continue to attract more than a half million people a year. They come to eat their fill of hickory-smoked sliced beef, ribs, sausage, ham, salami, chicken, and turkey, served as sandwiches or by the plate.

Angelo, who died in 1997, passed on all his barbecue know-how to his son, Skeet, who has worked at the restaurant since he was sixteen. Skeet, now manager, is training his son, Jason, to some day take over the restaurant.

Many of Angelo's old hunting trophies—a buffalo, deer, reindeer, antelope and more—adorn the walls at Angelo's. During the sixties, the buffalo head disappeared, then mysteriously was returned. An anonymous phone call, it seems, guided Angelo to an abandoned building. There he found his kidnapped buffalo with a note in its ear: "It looks good in my den, but it looks better at your place."

Gettin' there: From I-35 W North, take Northside Drive exit and go west. Northside becomes University Drive when it crosses Highway 199. Continue about one mile on University to White Settlement Road and turn left. Or from I-30, take University Drive exit and go north about one mile to White Settlement Road. Turn right.

Angelo's
2533 White Settlement Rd.
Fort Worth, TX 76107
817/332-0357

Cattlemen's Fort Worth Steak House
formerly Cattlemen's Steak House (1947)

Like a lot of success stories, the internationally acclaimed Cattlemen's Fort Worth Steak House, located in Fort Worth's Stockyards District, started almost by accident. The restaurant's story begins in Austin where attorney Jesse Roach and his wife, Mozelle, lived back in the forties. Jesse practiced law, and the couple also owned an insurance agency that sold policies to long-haul truck drivers.

"On one of Jesse's trips to Fort Worth to represent some truckers before a Texas Railroad Commission hearing, he drove out by the stockyards and was amazed by the number of trucks coming into Fort Worth," Mozelle wrote in a short memoir. "He came home with the idea that we should have a branch office for our insurance agency in Fort Worth." It wasn't long before the couple bought a vacant lot on North Main Street and built an office. In 1946 they moved both their business and home to Fort Worth and used the Austin location as a branch office.

The next year Jesse traveled to the Panhandle community of Higgins and met with a customer who owned a fleet of trucks and a small cafe. During their conversations, the man mentioned that he'd always wanted to run a cafe in Fort Worth. Well, Jesse suggested, how about looking at an empty building next to the agency? By the next day, the man had driven to Fort Worth and signed a lease. His new cafe had been open only a month or so when a tornado plowed through Higgins. Sadly, the man decided he could not repair his property back home and still stay in business in Fort Worth. So Jesse and Mozelle canceled his lease and bought the restaurant's equipment.

At first, the couple thought they'd lease the cafe to someone else. Then Jesse, intrigued with the restaurant business for a long time, decided he'd take it over. So he quit law and turned the insurance agency over to his wife. "It seemed as if every few days he was remodeling something or adding something to improve the business," Mozelle wrote. Soon the

23

restaurant became known for great barbecue, but Jesse didn't stop there. He wanted his place to be more than "just another cafe." With the goal of establishing a top-notch steak house, he and Mozelle traveled across the country and found producers who could supply aged, corn-fed beef.

The rest, as they say, is history.

Jesse died in 1988. Mozelle ran the business as an absentee owner until 1994 when a group of restaurateurs purchased it and changed the name to "Cattlemen's Fort Worth Steak House."

Today, customers line up at the door and wait for a table in one of the restaurant's three dining rooms. Once seated, they can mosey up to a glass display case, pick out a steak from a selection on ice, and watch the friendly chef char-broil it to their taste. Among the twelve different cuts featured on the menu are the 13-ounce "K.C. Strip Sirloin," the 16-ounce "Heart O' Texas Ribeye Steak," and the 9-ounce "Rose O' Texas Tenderloin."

Besides beef, the steak house also cooks up lobster tail, barbecue shrimp, fried shrimp and chicken, lamb fries, chicken-fried steak, and, of course, desserts (homemade pies and cheesecake).

The Cattlemen's at night, as seen from Main Street.

For customers hankering for more K.C. strip sirloins or Rose O' Texas tenderloins, the restaurant's "Air Mail Steaks" business ships meat across the country.

Not bad for an accidental success story.

Gettin' there: From North Freeway I-35W, exit Highway 183 (Northeast 28th Street) and turn west. Go 2 miles on NE 28th Street; turn south on North Main Street (Highway 287).

Cattlemen's Steak House
2458 N. Main St.
Fort Worth, TX 76106
817/624-3945
Website: www.cattlemenssteakhouse.com

Stop by and see: The Stockyards Collection and Museum at 131 E. Exchange Ave. houses photos and memorabilia from the stockyards' early days.

Ribs

2 cases ribs
1 coffee cup paprika
1 ½ teaspoon black pepper
4 cups Liquid Smoke, divided

Mix ingredients listed, using only 2 cups Liquid Smoke. This is your rub. Lightly salt both sides of ribs. Then, using a brush, spread the mix on both sides of the ribs. Let sit for 5 minutes. Pour remaining 2 cups Liquid Smoke in water pan of the smoker. Add water so pan is ¾ full. Fill the wood chip box with chips, place in smoker. Preheat smoker to 250 degrees. Put ribs on skewer (10 ribs per skewer). Cook 2 hours, then check the thickest one to see if done. You will usually have to cook the ribs for another 30 minutes.

Joe T. Garcia's
(1935)

Say the name Joe T.'s around the Metroplex, and local folks know exactly what you're talking about. That's Joe T.'s, as in great Mexican food. Joe T. Garcia's Mexican Restaurant, to be precise.

Joe and Jesse Garcia opened their little cafe on the Fourth of July in 1935. Back then, the place seated sixteen people in one room. As the years went by, the Garcias, assisted by their five children, earned the devotion of more and more customers, and the business grew steadily. In 1953 Joe died. Undaunted, Jesse and her youngest daughter, Hope, took over. By the 1970s Joe T. Garcia's had established itself as one of the most popular restaurants in the Dallas-Fort Worth area.

To accommodate the increasing number of guests, the family built more dining rooms. They also added an outdoor pool and landscaped courtyards. Today, the local landmark seats more than 1,000 people. Amazingly, the tables, both indoors and out, fill up for lunch and dinner, a testament to its popularity and longstanding reputation for good food.

Though Joe T.'s restaurant building has changed, the menu hasn't. What menu there is. Customers have two choices— enchiladas or fajitas (beef and chicken). "The Dinner," Joe T.'s traditional platter, comes with tortilla chips and hot sauce, two cheese nachos, two cheese enchiladas, rice, beans, two beef tacos, guacamole, and homemade tortillas. Weekend diners who come for brunch can choose from a few more Tex-Mex offerings, such as huevos rancheros, migas, and menudo.

Besides Joe T.'s, the Garcia family operates a small neighborhood restaurant called Esperanza's Bakery and Cafe. The venture, begun to create jobs for other family members, later led to more businesses—a wholesale bread company and a mail-order salsa company.

Though the Garcias are proud of their many achievements, one prestigious honor stands above the rest. In 1998 Joe T.'s was one of eight American restaurants named as a "best grass-roots restaurant" in the annual James Beard Foundation awards for culinary excellence, the Oscar's equivalent for the restaurant industry.

As if anyone needed a reason to eat at Joe T.'s in the first place.

Gettin' there: Heading west from Mid-Cities or Dallas on I-30, exit University Drive (TCU area) and turn left/north. (If you go by the Fort Worth Zoo, you're going the wrong way.) Follow University for several miles. University becomes Northside Drive. Turn left on North Main. Turn right on 22nd Street. Joe T.'s is the corner of 22nd and Commerce.

Joe T. Garcia's
2201 Commerce St.
Fort Worth, TX 76106
817/626-4356
Website: www.joets.com

Stop by and see: Head downtown and see the Water Garden at Commerce and 15th Streets (near the convention center). The park features pools, waterfalls, channels, and fountains.

Carne Asada

2 pounds beef tenderloin
3 to 4 medium garlic cloves, peeled and crushed
2 teaspoons freshly ground black pepper
½ teaspoon cumin
¼ cup olive oil
salt

Slice the tenderloin lengthwise, with the grain, about ¼-inch thick. Combine all ingredients and toss with sliced beef. Marinate in the refrigerator at least 3 hours. Preheat a grill or heavy skillet. Cook for 2 to 4 minutes per side. Serves 6.

Guacamole

2 ripe Haas avocados
½ small white onion, finely chopped
1 tomato, finely chopped
1 serrano chile, seeded and minced
⅓ cup finely chopped cilantro

1 tablespoon fresh lemon juice
salt to taste

Halve the avocados. Remove seed, scoop out avocado meat
and mash with a fork. Add onion, tomato, serrano, cilantro,
lemon juice, and salt. Mix well. Serves 4.

Huevos Rancheros
2 tablespoons vegetable oil
4 corn tortillas
4 large eggs
2 cups Salsa Ranchera

In hot oil over medium-high heat, fry tortillas on both sides
until crisp. Drain on paper towels. Fry eggs sunny side up
and place on tortillas. Cover the eggs with warm ranchera
sauce and serve immediately.

Serves 2.

Salsa Ranchera:
2 serrano chilies
2 tomatoes
$\frac{1}{2}$ clove garlic, peeled
1 tablespoon vegetable oil
$\frac{1}{4}$ onion, minced
salt

Cook whole serranos in a hot skillet until toasted on all
sides. Puree the tomatoes, chilies, and garlic in a food processor. Heat oil, add onion, and cook until soft. Add tomato
puree and cook for 5 minutes, until sauce thickens. Add salt
to taste. Makes about 2 cups.

Paris Coffee Shop
(1926)

The story behind the Paris Coffee Shop in Fort Worth actually
starts in Greece. That's where an ambitious young man by the
name of Gregory Acikis was born in 1900. At the age of

thirteen or fourteen, he left his troubled homeland, boarded a boat, and headed for a new life in the United States. Gregory landed in New York, then worked his way southwest until he reached Fort Worth. Fearing discrimination because of his foreign surname, he changed it to a plain vanilla one—Smith. To earn money, Gregory Smith worked hard washing dishes at local restaurants. He sent what cash he could to his family in Greece. Later, he wrestled professionally to supplement his income. Within a few years, he had saved enough money to buy his own coffee shop downtown.

Meanwhile, in 1926, another man with a somewhat foreign name—Vic Paris—opened a coffee shop on Hemphill Street south of downtown. He called it the Paris Coffee Shop. Four years later, he sold the business to Gregory, who turned it into a thriving, popular establishment. Along the way, Gregory acquired a wife, then seven sons. Mike, the last one, arrived in 1943. As a boy, he often worked in his father's cafe, peeling fruit and slicing vegetables. Encouraged by the elder Smith to pursue an education, Mike earned an administrative management degree from North Texas State University. In 1965, three months into his work on a graduate degree, he learned his father had Parkinson's, a degenerative neurological disease. Mike dropped his classes and temporarily returned home to run the family business. Or so he thought. "Temporarily" stretched to 1971 when Gregory died. Mike decided to stay and keep the Paris Coffee Shop going. Three years later, when Hemphill Street was widened, he moved the restaurant to an empty grocery store across the street. His devoted clientele willingly followed.

These days, the cafe at noon feeds more than 700 customers, many of whom Mike can call by name. Most of them know the daily specials by heart—fish on Wednesdays and Fridays, baked short ribs on Tuesdays, and chicken and dumplings on Thursdays. The specials come with tea or coffee, hot rolls and corn bread plus choice of two or three vegetables, like green beans, mashed potatoes, spinach, pinto beans, macaroni and cheese, and creamed cauliflower. Besides homemade pies and breads, Mike also sells a lot of cookies. HIS cookies. Every morning he bakes about fifteen dozen in six varieties, including gourmet chocolate chip, white chocolate chip pecan, oatmeal raisin pecan, peanut butter chocolate chip pecan, German chocolate and coconut haystack macaroons, and chocolate white chocolate chip.

Breakfast? The Paris Coffee Shop does that, too. No doughnuts here, but there's plenty of cinnamon rolls, blueberry muffins, biscuits, and Belgium waffles.

In recent years, a third-generation Smith joined the ranks at the cafe. Mike's son, Troy, who as a boy bused tables and washed dishes for his father, these days fields kitchen emergencies, greets customers, and keeps things running smoothly around the place. And when the time comes, yes, he'll keep the Paris Coffee Shop tradition going.

As they say, like grandfather, like father, like son.

Gettin' there: From I-35, take the Rosedale exit. Go west on Rosedale. At Hemphill and Rosedale, go south. The Paris Coffee Shop is located at the corner of Magnolia and Hemphill.

Paris Coffee Shop
704 W. Magnolia Ave.
Fort Worth, TX 76104
817/335-2041

Egg Custard Pie

5 eggs
1 cup sugar
2 cups milk
1 ounce butter
1 ½ teaspoons vanilla
one 10-inch pie shell, unbaked

Scald milk and butter.

Mix eggs, sugar, and vanilla together with a wire whip.

Pour scalded milk into egg mixture. Beat with a wire whip until frothy on top. Pour into a pie shell, making sure the froth is on top of pie. Place in a preheated 375-degree oven. [Hint: preheat oven at 450 degrees and turn back to 375 when the pie is placed inside. It will bake while the oven cools down.] Bake about 25 minutes.

Every oven cooks differently. Check when the pie filling sets and is brown. It should be done. Do not overcook or filling will become watery.

▪▪▪▪▪▪▪▪▪▪▪▪▪▪▪▪▪▪▪▪▪▪▪

Irving

Big State Drug's Fountain and Grill (1948)

Returning to the old-time restaurants of your past makes you feel good, right? If you're old enough, sitting at a stool or booth at a soda fountain in a drugstore will likely trigger the same warm fuzzies. I'm forty-something, and I can remember eating a hamburger with my mother at Nichol's Pharmacy and the Stonewall Drug Store in northwest Corpus Christi, where I grew up. Sadly, those two soda fountains are long gone. But, thank goodness, a few neighborhood drugstores across Texas have survived, in spite of big-name drug and department stores (I won't name names). Big State Drug's Fountain and Grill in Irving is one.

In the early 1900s a haberdashery (a business that sells small wares and notions) originally occupied the building at 100 E. Irving Blvd. Some time later, the haberdashery changed into a drugstore and became Big State Drug in 1948, which it's been ever since. To date, Big State is one of only two drugstores in Dallas County that still has a soda fountain and grill.

At the counter, you can order breakfast from 8 to 11 A.M. Eggs, omelettes, pancakes, grits, biscuits with gravy, and French toast are just a few of the morning favorites at Big State. For lunch, if you're extra hungry, try the Texas Tombstone, a burger with two all-beef patties, bacon, cheese, lettuce, and tomato. There's also double hamburgers and cheeseburgers. Plus triple burgers ("you better be hungry!" the menu warns) and triple cheeseburgers ("three patties, three cheeses, HOLY COW!" exclaims the menu). BLTs, chicken and tuna salad, ham, turkey, fried egg, and chicken-fried steak are just a few of the sandwich choices at Big State. You can also order chicken strips, steak fingers, chicken-fried steak, and chopped steak, all served with fries, Texas toast, and gravy.

And now for my favorite part . . . the fountain specialties at Big State. They include creamy shakes and malts, heavenly floats, soothing sundaes, huge banana splits, old-fashioned sodas, and ice cream cones. Just the thought of a frothy chocolate malt makes me glad that Big State Drug's Fountain and Grill and the other last surviving soda fountains have withstood the test of time.

Now let's order!

Gettin' there: Big State Drug can be easily accessed two ways. Via Texas 183, exit south on O'Connor Road to Irving Boulevard and turn left. Or via the lightrail train from downtown Dallas.

The DART Trinity Express stops in downtown Irving. From the train station, just walk south on Hastings or Ohio (the station is located in between these) approximately one block to Irving Boulevard and turn left.

Big State Drug's Fountain and Grill
100 E. Irving Blvd.
Irving, TX 75060
972/254-1521

Stop by and see: Today's trivia question: what famous funny man began as a high school cheerleader in his hometown of Waco, Texas? Answer: Steve Martin. You'll learn all sorts of interesting tidbits about Hollywood when you tour the Studios at Las Colinas at 6301 N. O'Connor Rd. (Building One). The facility is a working high-tech motion picture and television sound stage.

Soda jerks at Big State gladly give customers the metal mixing canister so they can slurp up every last drop of shake.

Famous Big State Drug Chocolate Malt
Place 2½ scoops of Blue Bell Premium Milk Chocolate ice cream in a metal canister. Add two good squirts of chocolate syrup, then fill to top of ice cream with milk. Add 2-3 scoopfuls of powdered malt. Blend well with mixer. Serve in stemmed malt glass.

Jacksboro

Green Frog Restaurant
(1928)

Ah, the good ol' days. I remember penny candy, marbles and jacks, and black-and-white television. For folks in Jacksboro, memories of the good ol' days include meals at the Green Frog Restaurant, where burgers once cost a dime and a full lunch went for two bits. Those prices date back to 1928, when Emma and George Weaver originally opened the restaurant next door to the old Fort Richardson Hotel.

"We were about to starve to death," Emma retorted matter-of-factly when asked by the local newspaper why they decided to start the business.

You might wonder about a place called the "Green Frog," a rather unusual name for a restaurant. The story goes that a friend, Pick Hensley, suggested the name. At the same time, he struck a deal with the Weavers. In exchange for making a new sign for the Green Frog, he asked that Ma feed him hamburgers until he was full. She agreed. So Pick constructed the sign, and Ma cooked him burgers. Three of them.

The Weavers' son, Tobe, ran the restaurant for a long time. Other owners came and went. In 1982 Billy Bullard bought the Green Frog and has been running it ever since.

These days hamburgers at the Green Frog cost $2.50. Besides burgers, the restaurant also serves chicken-fried steak, grilled pork chops, fried chicken, steaks, Mexican plates, sandwiches, soups, and salads.

And yes, in case you're wondering, the Green Frog does serve fried frog legs.

Gettin' there: Jacksboro is located 70 miles northwest of Fort Worth on U.S. 281.

Green Frog Restaurant
416 N. Main St.
Jacksboro, TX 76458
940/567-3724

Stop by and see: Texas history comes alive at Fort Richardson State Historical Park, which preserves the remains of this northernmost federal fort established after the Civil War. Built in 1867, the fort was a strategic post in the campaign against Indian harassment of travelers and settlers.

This tastes great with the Green Frog's soft-serve ice cream.

Bread Pudding

5 eggs, beaten
3 cups bread, cubed
2 cups sugar
½ gallon milk
2 tablespoons vanilla
¼ cup melted butter
1 cup raisins, optional

Mix together. Spray a medium-sized baking pan. Bake at 350 degrees for 30-35 minutes. Consistency will be close to an egg custard.

Lubbock

Doll House Cafe
(1930s)

If the local Texas Rangers eat at the Doll House Cafe, then you know the food's got to be good. In fact, they rarely miss the chicken and dumplings special on Tuesdays or beans and corn bread on Fridays.

Owner Serena Mankins guesstimates that the cafe dates back to the 1930s. Many of her customers have been dining there for years, some of whom go back several generations.

The breakfast menu features the standard morning fare: eggs, sausage, biscuits, pancakes, French toast, omelets, and oatmeal. For lunch, there're burgers, sandwiches, stew, chili, Frito pie, steak finger baskets, and more.

"Our most famous menu items are the chicken and dumplings," she says. "Also meat loaf, pot roast, chicken-fried steak, and, of course, desserts."

"The coconut cream pie is our best seller," Serena continues. "Chocolate cream is second." The cooks know the recipes—top-secret ones that stay within the Mankins family—so well that they rarely, if ever, measure the ingredients.

Bet the Texas Rangers can tell you that the pies at the Doll House are just as good as those chicken and dumplings.

Gettin' there: From I-27, exit Texas 62 and go west. On Avenue K, turn north.

Doll House Cafe
1717 Ave. K
Lubbock, TX 79401
806/762-4665

Stop by and see: The Ranching Heritage Center, part of the Museum of Texas Tech University (Fourth Street and Indiana Avenue), preserves 33 authentic ranching structures spread across a 14-acre tract. The restored buildings, all moved from various sites and ranches across the state, chronologically trace the evolution of Texas's ranching culture and customs from the 1840s to the 1920s.

Pecan Pie
3 eggs, slightly beaten
1 cup sugar
1 teaspoon vanilla
1 cup butter pecan syrup
1 cup chopped pecans (no halves)
1 unbaked pie shell

Mix ingredients in order listed. Pour into pie shell. Bake at 350 degree for 45-50 minutes. Top should be crunchy when done.

Chicken-Fried Steak

6-8 tenderized beef cutlets
I cup buttermilk
2 eggs, well beaten
seasoned flour
oil for frying

Beat eggs; add buttermilk. Dip cutlets in flour, then egg mixture, then again in flour. Fry in hot oil, ½-inch deep, for 5-6 minutes on each side. Drain on paper towels. Enjoy.

Muenster

Rohmer's Restaurant
(1959)

Land agents Emil and August Flusche in 1889 founded the little town of Muenster, named for the capital of their native Westphalia, Germany. In 1953 another man with German roots, Emil Rohmer, opened the Ace Cafe. Six years later he and his wife, Agnes, moved the business across the street into a stone house and renamed it Rohmer's Restaurant. Emil's gone now, but his namesake hasn't stopped serving the same good food.

Though Emil used to serve German fare only once a month (so the locals wouldn't tire of it), the menu these days regularly offers it. Take your pick from wiener schnitzel (a breaded and sauteed pork cutlet), chicken schnitzel, bratwurst, smoked pork sausage, reuben sandwich, chicken schnitzel sandwich, or sausage on a bun, served with German potato salad and sauerkraut. Rohmer's also serves a variety of other foods—steaks, chicken-fried steaks, soup and salads, six different burgers, ten kinds of sandwiches, fried fish and shrimp, chicken (fried and marinated; livers and gizzards, too), barbecue (pork ribs and beef brisket), and two Mexican dishes (enchiladas and chili).

Gettin' there: Muenster is 73 miles north of Fort Worth.

Rohmer's Restaurant
217 E. Division
Muenster, TX 76252
940/759-2973

Coconut Cream Pie

2 cups milk
¾ cup sugar
3 egg yolks
2 tablespoons cornstarch
dash salt
1 teaspoon vanilla
1 cup shredded coconut
one pie shell

Cook milk, sugar, egg yolks, cornstarch, and salt until thick. Add vanilla and coconut. Pour into a baked pie shell.

Meringue

3 egg whites
¼ cup sugar
¼ teaspoon cream of tartar

Whip until meringue peaks. Spoon onto pie. Top with coconut.

Copper Penny Salad

2 pounds carrots, sliced, cooked, cooled
I can whole kernel corn, drained
I onion, sliced
I bell pepper, sliced
I can tomato soup
¾ cup sugar
½ cup vinegar
¼ cup oil
I tablespoon mustard (the real stuff)
I tablespoon Worcestershire sauce

Mix and chill.

Plano

Poor Richard's Café
formerly Park Mall Coffee Shop (1973)

Here's some food for thought: "We're best to ourselves when we're good to others." And another bite to ponder... "We make a living by what we get and a life by what we give."

You'll find more sage advice and thought-provoking proverbs when you visit Poor Richard's Café in Plano. They're hung in frames on the café's walls and scattered throughout the extensive menu. The unusual "trademarks" are the brainchild of owner Richard Butterly. In 1982 he bought the former Park Mall Coffee Shop, which originally opened in 1973, and renamed it Poor Richard's. The new name came from both his teaching background and his childhood. As a high school teacher, he often used quotations and proverbs from *Poor Richard's Almanac* in the classroom. The other reason he named his café Poor Richard's is... well, because when he was growing up, his family was always poor.

Not anymore. Richard and his namesake do a booming business. Every morning, tables at the Plano restaurant fill up,

39

mostly with local menfolk who come to order breakfast, drink coffee, and talk shop. Lots of fried eggs and Southern grits get eaten here. Poor Richard's also serves up a hearty selection of pancakes, waffles, and omelettes, including a barbecue omelette with chicken, sauteed mushrooms, and onions.

At noon many of the same regular customers return for lunch. "Home-cooked" specials vary by the day. Mondays, for instance, feature fried chicken, while turkey and dressing are served on Thursdays. You can also choose from a long list of "lunch platters," served every day (like chicken-fried chicken, grilled pork chops, sliced roast beef, and fried catfish). Burgers, sandwiches, soups, salads, and appetizers round out the menu.

And by the way, here's a closing bit of wisdom from Poor Richard: "When you're through changing, you're through."

Well put, Richard.

Gettin' there: Located on the southeast corner of Park Boulevard and Avenue K. East of Central Expressway.

Poor Richard's Café
2442 Avenue K
Plano, TX 75074
972/423-1524

Ponder

Ranchman's Cafe
(1948)

Life's slow and easy in the small town of Ponder. At least, that's what the menu at Ranchman's claims. And any place with a creaky screened door out front can't be all wrong. Folks have been traipsing through the door since 1948 when Grace "Pete" Jackson originally opened the Ranchman's Cafe (dubbed locally as the Ponder Steakhouse). Her down-home meals quickly won a regular following of appetites, and word spread to nearby Dallas and Fort Worth that her hand-cut sirloins, T-bones, and chicken-fried steaks were worth the drive. After her retirement, Pete sold the cafe but visited regularly until her death at the age of 93 in 1998.

At Ranchman's, the atmosphere is pretty laid back. Oh, there's a few rules. "We will not separate checks, except at the register," the menu warns. And if you want a baked potato with your steak, then you'll have to call ahead. Otherwise, pull up a chair to one of the vintage dinette tables. It's time to EAT.

If a grilled steak doesn't suit you, Ranchman's also serves quail, grilled chicken breast, ham, chicken strips, and a fine selection of sandwiches and burgers. Blink twice, and you may miss the breakfast menu, listed between the sandwiches and drinks. It offers ham, bacon, or sausage served with two eggs, toast, and hash browns or grits. And pies? Of course, the Ranchman's got those. Cobblers, too.

On the front of the menu, a notice advises, "large print and Braille menus available." Isn't that unusual for a restaurant? "My degree was in special education and speech therapy," explains owner Dave Ross. "So I'm sensitive to the varied needs of different people. I always look for disabled people to give them opportunities to work."

Any place with a creaky screened door out front and an owner like Dave has to be pretty special.

Gettin' there: Ranchman's is located on West Bailey St. (Ponder's main street), a half block west of FM 156. Ponder is located 10 miles north of Texas 114, four miles south of U.S. 380, and six miles west of I-35W. Take the Ponder exit (FM 2449).

Ranchman's Cafe
110 W. Bailey
Ponder, TX 76259
940/479-2221
Website: www.ranchman.com
email: ranchman@iglobal.net

Ranchman's Buttermilk Pie

2 eggs, beaten
1 cup sugar
1 cup buttermilk
½ stick margarine
2 tablespoons flour
1 teaspoon lemon flavoring
½ teaspoon vanilla

Beat the eggs separately. Melt the butter. Stir in the flour. Add lemon flavoring. Add vanilla, buttermilk, sugar, and beaten eggs. Mix well and pour into an unbaked piecrust. Bake at 350 degrees for 30 minutes.

Ranchman's Caramel Pie

3 egg yolks
2½ cups milk
1½ cups sugar
½ stick margarine
½ cup flour
1 teaspoon vanilla

In a small saucepan over medium heat, heat ½ cup sugar to caramelize. Stir constantly and bring to a simmer. Be careful not to burn the sugar. In a medium saucepan, melt the margarine. Stir in the flour, mix thoroughly. In a medium bowl, beat the eggs. Add milk and remaining sugar. Beat in margarine and flour mixture. Add the caramelized sugar and vanilla. Stir and stir and stir. This filling gets really thick! Pour into an unbaked piecrust. Top with meringue. Bake at 350 degrees until the meringue is a nice caramel color (about 15 minutes).

Ranchman's Southern Pecan Pie

3 egg yolks
3 cups sugar
3 cups white corn syrup
1 teaspoon vanilla
½ stick margarine
whole pecans

Beat together yolks, sugar, and syrup. Add vanilla and margarine. Mix thoroughly. Place two layers of whole pecans in three unbaked pie shells. Pour sugar mixture over pecans. Cook at 350 degree for 30 minutes or until centers are set.

Salado

Stagecoach Inn
(1860s)

Salado is one of those quaint places in Texas where you go to escape life, have fun with friends, and spend some money. I know. I've done all three here. On a Saturday night several years ago, Lisa Bosch, Debbie Reed, and I forsook our families (with the husbands' permission, naturally), fled to Salado, and treated ourselves to a weekend off. The retreat included a sumptuous dinner at the famous Stagecoach Inn and an overnight stay at the adjoining motel. It was time and money well invested.

W.B. Armstrong, one of the area's first settlers, built the inn in the 1860s. Back then, it was called the Shady Villa Hotel. According to the restaurant's brown paper place mats, a lot of famous folks—Sam Houston, Gen. George Custer, Charles Goodnight, Jesse James, and Sam Bass—ate and slept at the Shady Villa, located along the well-traveled Chisholm Trail. The names of all guests were recorded in the inn's register, which—alas—was stolen in 1944 and never seen again. In the early forties Mr. and Mrs. Dion Van Bibber restored the frame building and renamed it the Stagecoach Inn. In 1959 Bill and Betty Bratton purchased the inn, modernized it, and added a two-story hotel.

Today the food and historic ambience attract most people to the Stagecoach Inn for lunch and supper. Menus don't exist in the restaurant. Never have. The story goes that waitresses way back when never knew what time the stagecoach was due so they'd recite the day's few offerings after everyone arrived. The tradition continues to this day, but the staff have more to remember—twelve entrees!

An evening visit starts with a cup of chicken consommé, a basket of hush puppies, and a run-down of the evening's main courses. The restaurant's more popular offerings include roast prime rib of beef, a 6-ounce filet, grilled chicken breast, and chicken-fried steak. All come with a baked potato, two vegetables, and dinner muffins. While orders are prepared, the waitress serves your choice of salads—tossed green, fresh fruit, or tomato aspic. Dessert comes with the meal, too. The inn's signature delicacy is a strawberry kiss, a meringue shell filled with ice cream and topped with strawberries. Fudge pecan pie and French lemon pie also deserve a round of applause.

Crispy hushpuppies, prime rib, fudge pecan pie. . . . I think we deserve another weekend off. What do you say, Lisa and Debbie?

Gettin' there: On Interstate 35, exit Salado. Reservations recommended.

Stagecoach Inn
1 Main St.
Salado, TX 76571
254/947-9400
800/732-8994
Website: http://touringtexas.com/stage

Stop by and see: Shop and walk 'til you drop. Salado has lots of interesting and fun shops along tree-shaded Main Street.

Banana Fritters

2 cups flour
$\frac{1}{4}$ teaspoon salt
1 tablespoon baking powder
$\frac{1}{2}$ cup sugar
$\frac{1}{2}$ cup oil
2 eggs
6 to 8 large bananas

Mix dry ingredients with enough milk to make a medium thick batter. Add eggs and oil, beat until smooth. Cut bananas into 2-inch lengths and split lengthwise. Dip into batter, turning until well coated. Fry in hot oil until brown.

Sprinkle with powdered sugar and top with a maraschino cherry.

Barbecued Chicken

3-pound frying chicken
3 medium-sized onions, sliced thin

Cut the chicken lengthwise or in quarters. Arrange in single layers, skin side up in roasting pan. Sprinkle with salt and pepper. Pour in enough hot water to cover bottom of pan. Arrange onion slices over chicken; stick some under wings and legs. Bake uncovered 30 minutes at 350 degrees. Then turn chicken on other side and bake 30 minutes longer. Remove from oven and pour off all but $\frac{3}{4}$ cup of liquid in bottom of pan. Turn skin side up and pour barbecue sauce (recipe follows) over chicken and return to oven. Bake at 350 degrees for one hour or until fork shows chicken is done. Baste frequently.

Barbecue Sauce

$1\frac{1}{2}$ cups tomato juice
$\frac{1}{4}$ teaspoon cayenne pepper
2 teaspoons salt
$\frac{1}{4}$ teaspoon pepper
$\frac{1}{4}$ teaspoon powdered mustard
$4\frac{1}{2}$ teaspoons Worcestershire sauce
1 bay leaf
1 teaspoon sugar
$\frac{1}{2}$ cup cider vinegar
3 peeled garlic cloves, minced
3 tablespoons butter

Combine and simmer 10 minutes.

Texas Historical Marker Stagecoach Inn

Constructed during the 1860s, the Stagecoach Inn was known as Salado Hotel and as Shady Villa before the current name was adopted in 1943. Military figures George Armstrong Custer and Robert E. Lee and cattle baron Shanghai Pierce are among those thought to have stayed here. A good example of frontier vernacular architecture, the Stagecoach Inn features a two-story galleried porch with a second-story balustrade.

Sherman

Juicy Pig Cafe
(1936)

Juicy Pig's story starts in a 'roundabout way, like several in this book. It gets a little complicated, too, unless you can keep the names all straight.

It starts with a man by the name of Joe Nelson, who was running a place in Sherman called the Red Bird Inn. When residents voted in beer in the early thirties, another man, Anthony McCrue, decided he wanted to start a new business. He and Joe struck a 50-50 deal and built the Juicy Pig Cafe in 1936. A third man by the name of Coy Knox worked for the business partners. Then war erupted. Joe joined the Navy, and Coy went into the Field Airborne. After a year and one day in the military, a doctor told Knox to find an "easy" job. Back home, the Juicy

Pig had closed down, but Anthony told him that he could run it. After four years, Anthony generously gave the business to Coy and his wife. The couple ran the cafe for 35 years and then retired.

The Juicy Pig has changed hands twice since the Knoxes. It also moved from South Travis Street to its current location on South Sam Rayburn Street.

Breakfast here features a favorite 1940s recipe of creamed eggs (hard-boiled eggs in a cheddar cheese sauce)on toast or biscuits. Egg sandwiches and omelets are among the other choices. For lunch, the Juicy Pig, which bills some of its cuisine as "German-American," always serves daily specials that change every week. They might include breaded chicken breast (served with mushrooms, mashed potatoes and a salad), a hot reuben sandwich with French fries, schnitzel cordon bleu topped with melted ham and cheese (served with pasta and a salad), and German meat loaf. Customers also can choose from burgers, a variety of sandwiches, chicken-fried steak, German sausage, and pork chops.

Gettin' there: From I-75, take the Park and Center Street exit (Exit 57). The Juicy Pig is on the west side of the interstate.

Juicy Pig Cafe
1604 S. Sam Rayburn Frway.
Sherman, TX 75091
903/870-1603

Stop by and see: If you're a romantic at heart, then you'll definitely want to visit the C.S. Roberts House at 915 S. Crockett St. One of the home's owners, Charles Stanly Roberts, fell in love with his wife on Jan. 7, 1905. He proposed a year to the day later, and the two married Nov. 7, 1906. Thereafter, he faithfully presented his wife with a present on the seventh day of each month. Now that's romantic!

Creamed Eggs in Cheddar Cheese Sauce

Make a roux out of unbleached flour and butter. In a separate pan, warm up heavy cream and half-and-half. Add roux and bring to a slow boil. Remove from heat and add finely cut-up sharp cheddar cheese. Add chopped, hard-boiled eggs. Mix well and serve over toast, biscuits, or corn bread. Salt and pepper to taste, and add a little garlic powder.

Wiener Schnitzel

4-5 ounce pork cutlet, butterflied

Pound thin with meat cleaver. Salt and pepper to taste. Dip in well-beaten egg, then coat with bread crumbs. Pan fry. We serve this with home fries and a mixed salad.

Temple

Bluebonnet Cafe
(1948)

The Bluebonnet Cafe originally opened sometime in the late 1920s or early thirties. Laverne Pitts, who took over the restaurant on the old Austin highway with her husband, J.C., in 1948, isn't sure of the exact year. But one of the earliest listings she found for the Bluebonnet in the Temple telephone book was 1933. Sadly, J.C. died in '83. All these years later, Laverne has barely slowed down and still greets customers faithfully.

"Leo, how are you?" she asked a man sitting on a stool at the counter. Later, after he had eaten his lunch and left, Laverne got a bit worried. "Did you serve Leo dessert?" she asked a waitress. "No, ma'am," the woman replied. Laverne asked two other waitresses the same question. Both shook their heads. More than likely, Leo received an extra serving of attention the next time he sat at his stool. That's the way Laverne treats folks at the Bluebonnet. She makes everyone feel special.

These days, her daughter and son-in-law, Susan and George Luck, own the Bluebonnet, which claims chicken-fried steak as its number one seller. The Texas favorite is a featured lunch special at least once a week. When I visited, the day's noon specials were chicken and dumplings, roast beef with brown gravy, and catfish fillets, all served with pinto beans, baked squash, diced potatoes, vegetable slaw, and apple cobbler. Though tempted, I ordered apple pie with Blue Bell vanilla ice cream. When Margie set the plate in front of me, I couldn't believe the size of the slice! The crust must have measured four inches across. Needless to say, I finished every last crumb of pie and drop of ice cream.

During my visit, I noticed that the size of the cafe's crisp, white napkins rival the generous-sized portions of pie. They're huge. According to Laverne, they're a tradition at the Bluebonnet.

"J.C. told me that the only way we'd make this place successful was to feed working people," she says. "And they don't want to eat at a place with candles and tablecloths. I said, 'OK. But would you let me do one thing? I'd like linen napkins.' He thought a moment, then said 'OK, but only for lunch and dinner. No breakfast.' So that was my one luxury item at the Bluebonnet." For more than 50 years, Martin Linen Supply Co. in Waco has supplied the restaurant with its trademark napkins. "We get a lot of compliments," Laverne says. One man said, "Food's good, the service is OK, but these linen napkins are worth coming in for!"

I'd say the majority of customers would disagree with him—the food's better than good at the Bluebonnet Cafe. It's downright delicious.

Gettin' there: From I-35, exit Avenue H and 57th Street. Go east on Avenue H. Cross 31st Street. Turn left on 25th Street. Cafe's on the right, across the street from the Scott and White Santa Fe Medical Center.

Bluebonnet Cafe
705 S. 25th St.
Temple, TX 76504
254/773-6654

Stop by and see: Since I'm a bit partial to state parks (my husband manages one), I'd recommend you visit the very first one in Texas—Mother Neff State Park. Isabella Eleanor Neff, the mother of Gov. Pat Neff, in 1916 donated six acres of land along the Leon River. Then other folks followed suit and gave land, too. The 259-acre park is located 15 miles northwest of Temple on Texas 36, then five miles north on Texas 236.

Glazed Carrots

bag of frozen baby carrots
sugar
salt

Cook carrots. Drain juice and pour into a saucepan. Add about $\frac{1}{4}$ cup sugar, a pinch of salt, and a little food coloring. Bring to a boil. Mix some cornstarch with a little cold water; add to sugar mixture and cook until thickened. Pour over carrots.

Egg Custard

4 cups milk
1 heaping cup sugar

Bring to a boil.

5 eggs, beaten well
$\frac{1}{2}$ teaspoon vanilla

When sugar and milk start to boil, add egg mixture. Pour into 9-inch unbaked pie shell. Sprinkle nutmeg on top. Bake at 350 degrees, about 30 minutes. Custard is done when it slightly wiggles in the center when gently shaken.

Doyle Phillips Steak House
(1958)

This Temple tradition has been in business for more than four decades. Doyle Phillips moved to the city from Hearne in 1955 to run the Greyhound Bus Station Cafeteria. Three years later he opened his steak house on South General Bruce Drive. Catfish and steaks are the specialty at this roadside restaurant. Today, Phillip's son-in-law, Douglas Keilers, owns the restaurant, and grandson, Ray Keilers, works as assistant manager.

Gettin' there: From northbound I-35, take Exit 398 or 399. From southbound, take Midway Drive exit and go under overpass and head north on the access road.

Doyle Phillips Steak House
4011 S. General Bruce Dr.
Interstate 35
Temple, TX 76502
254/778-9951

■■■■■■■■■■■■■■■■■■■■■■■■■

Other old-time restaurants:

Abilene
Dixie Pig Restaurant (1931)
1401 Butternut St.
Abilene, TX 79601
915/673-3292

Dallas
Campisi's Egyptian (1947)
5610 E. Mockingbird Lane
Dallas, TX 75206
214/827-0355

Royal Tokyo Japanese
Restaurant (1973)
7525 Greenville Ave.
Dallas, TX 75231
214/368-3304

Vern's Place (1966)
3600 Main St.
Dallas, TX 75226
214/823-0435

Denton
Tom and Jo's Café (1945)
702 S. Elm St.
Denton, TX 76201
940/387-0491

Fort Worth

Mexican Inn Cafe (1926)
516 Commerce St.
Fort Worth, TX 76102
817/332-2772

Star Cafe (1940s)
111 West Exchange
Fort Worth, TX 76106
817/624-8701

Grand Prairie

Isabella's Pizzeria (1979)
617 W. Marshall Dr.
Grand Prairie, TX 75051
972/262-5108

Millar Cafe and Soda
Fountain (1922)
(formerly Millar Drug)
106 W. Main St.
Grand Prairie, TX 75051
972/263-9924

Irving

Angelo's Spaghetti & Pizza House (1966)
1330 W. Pioneer Dr.
Irving, TX 75061
972/254-7242

Joe's Coffee Shop (1964)
425 W. Irving Blvd.
Irving, TX 75060
972/253-7335

Las Lomas Restaurant (1911)
2215 N. O'Connor Rd.
Irving, TX 75062
972/257-1898

Lamesa
Allen's Galley (about 1970)
920 N. Dallas
Lamesa, TX 79331
806/872-3411

Lubbock
Pancake House (1961)
510 Ave. Q
Lubbock, TX 79401
806/765-8506

Stephenville
Jake and Dorothy's Cafe (1948)
406 E. Washington St.
Stephenville, TX 76401
254/965-5211

Wichita Falls
Floral Heights Cafe (1930)
907 Van Buren St.
Wichita Falls, TX 76301
940/322-0577

Way down south

Aransas Pass

Bakery Cafe
(1929)

The Bakery Cafe in Aransas Pass is tucked into a row of store-fronts along South Commercial Street. So don't zip by too fast or you'll miss it.

"Steaks, seafood and Mexican food" touts the menu's cover. Truth is, the cafe serves lots more than that. Fried chicken, chicken-fried steaks, burgers, sandwiches, oyster stew, and chili are just a few of the offerings. The seafood specialty is the "Captain's Seafood Platter"—a deluxe assortment of fried oysters, shrimp, fish, and stuffed crab.

Breakfast is served all day ("except 11 A.M. to 2 P.M.," the menu hastens to add). Choose from omelettes, taquitos, hot cakes, French toast, and homemade biscuits with sausage gravy.

And what about the "bakery" part of the cafe's name? Well, don't worry. Every day, there's plenty of homemade pastries and pies to be had, such as doughnuts, sweet rolls, fruit pies, and cream pies.

Gettin' there: Aransas Pass is located approximately 20 miles northeast of Corpus Christi.

Bakery Cafe
434 S. Commercial St.
Aransas Pass, TX 78336
361/758-3511

Stop by and see: Ride the free ferry to Port Aransas. A fun adventure.

Blessing

Blessing Hotel Coffee Shop
(1906)

In the annals of eating across Texas, the Blessing Hotel Coffee Shop ranks high. It's been around for decades, probably since the old hotel was built in 1906 by rancher Jonathan Edwards Pierce.

The little town of Blessing sprang up around the turn of the century when the Southern Pacific Railroad came to Matagorda County. Pierce, who gave railway right-of-way through his ranch, was so happy about the train's arrival that he tried to name the community "Thank God," but postal officials wouldn't go for it. So Pierce offered up "Blessing," and they agreed. To accommodate the increasing number of travelers, he constructed the two-story clapboard Hotel Blessing. In contrast to Victorian-style buildings of the time, Blessing's hotel, which had 25 rooms, drew from the "Mission Revival" style of architecture. A faint resemblance to the Alamo is apparent in the second story's roofline and arched windows.

In the 1930s the hotel was refinished and painted. Room rental ceased in 1972. Five years later, Abel B. Pierce (Pierce's grandson) and his wife, Ruth, donated the old hotel to the Blessing Historical Foundation. It is listed in the National Register of Historic Places and is a designated Texas Historic Landmark.

For more than two decades, Helen Feldhousen has owned the restaurant business. "When I took over in 1977, the hotel was closed, but I don't think the coffee shop has ever closed," she says. "The hotel reopened in '79." Yep, you can rent a room again at the Hotel Blessing. They're comfortable but not fancy.

Whether you're staying the night or just passing through, plan to eat lunch at the Hotel Blessing Coffee Shop, even if you have to go out of your way to get here. Helen oversees the noon meals that put Blessing on the map—a help-yourself spread of comfort food piled in pots and pans set atop two antique stoves. Every day but Christmas the feast includes at least three main entrees, such as chicken-fried steak, roast beef, meat loaf, fried chicken, and fried fish. There're also plenty of vegetables, homemade bread, and tempting desserts, like peach cobbler, chocolate pie, and chocolate cake.

Many moons ago, customers used to traipse into the kitchen and heap their plates full from pots simmering on the stove. In 1981, though, the tradition stopped when the health department folks frowned on it. Though the stoves are in the dining room now, the same down-home atmosphere and old-time decor remain, making lunch at the Hotel Blessing Coffee Shop an experience you won't soon forget.

Gettin' there: Blessing is located at the intersection of Texas 35 and FM 616, about 13 miles north of Palacios. The hotel is at the corner of 10th Street and Avenue B.

Blessing Hotel Coffee Shop
FM 616 & 10th St.
Box 119

Blessing, TX 77419
361/588-6623

White Bread

4¼ cups warm water
¼ cup sugar
3 tablespoons shortening
5 teaspoons salt
3 packages yeast
12 cups flour

Put warm water in large bowl. Add sugar, shortening, salt, and yeast. Let sit 10 minutes. Add 4 cups flour and mix thoroughly. Add remaining flour gradually and mix to a dough that won't stick to hands. Knead 8-10 minutes. Place in greased bowl and let rise in warm place until doubled in bulk. Knead down and make 4 loaves. Place in greased pans. Let rise again until doubled in bulk. Bake in 350-degree oven for 45 minutes.

Dirty Rice

2 pounds ground meat
½ pound pork sausage
1 (10-ounce) can cream of celery soup
2 (10-ounce) cans cream of mushroom soup
2 soup cans of water
1 box dry onion soup mix
½ cup green onion, chopped
½ cup chopped onion
1¼ cups chopped celery
1 cup chopped bell pepper
3 cups uncooked rice
1 teaspoon salt
1 teaspoon red pepper
¼ teaspoon black pepper

Brown ground meat and sausage together. Stir in rest of ingredients. Place in a large pan or dish, and bake in oven 1 hour. Stir once during baking.

Peach Cobbler

4 cups flour
4 tablespoons baking powder
6 cups sugar

1 1-gallon can sliced peaches
1 pound butter

Melt butter in large baking pan. Then mix all ingredients together and put in pan. Bake at 350 degrees until brown.

Helen Feldhousen's Chocolate Pie

1 cup sugar
¼ cup flour
5 tablespoons cocoa
2 cups milk
3 egg yolks
1 teaspoon vanilla
1 tablespoon butter
1 baked 8-inch or 9-inch pie shell

Sift sugar, flour, and cocoa together. Add 1 cup of milk and mix. Then mix egg yolks in the other cup of milk and beat. Add egg and milk mixture to the first mixture. Cook in a double boiler until thick. Add vanilla and butter. Stir and pour into pie shell. Cook and put meringue on top.

Meringue

3 egg whites
7 tablespoons sugar

Beat egg whites until stiff. Add sugar gradually. Spread over pie. Brown at 350 degrees for 12 minutes.

Corpus Christi

Frank's Spaghetti House
(1947)

When I was a kid growing up in Corpus Christi, I loved to eat at Frank's Spaghetti House. The old restaurant, as its name implies, is literally housed in a HOUSE. A two-story, red-bricked one, to be precise, with a wide front porch. We always ordered pizza, and it came with a wine bottle filled with the restaurant's special sauce. Oh, that stuff made the pizza taste even BETTER!

Frank's Spaghetti House has been around since 1947 when the original Frank, a Sicilian, opened the business. Besides pizza and spaghetti, the restaurant has lots of Italian favorites such as lasagna, manicotti, veal Parmesan, chicken cacciatore, eggplant Parmesan, beef ravioli, fettucine Alfredo, and shrimp Parmesan.

And, oh, yes, the restaurant still serves that special sauce I remember so well, a tangy, garlicky Italian vinaigrette called Frank's House Dressing. Customers pour it on everything. The restaurant also sells the sauce by the bottle—recycled wine bottles, of course.

Some things, thank goodness, never change.

Gettin' there: From I-37, exit Nueces Bay, turn west. On Leopard Street, turn south. The restaurant is located on the east side at the corner of Leopard and Palm Streets.

Frank's Spaghetti House
2724 Leopard St.
Corpus Christi, TX 78408
361/882-0075

Stop by and see: The Texas State Aquarium on North Shoreline Boulevard exhibits more than 250 species of sea life in the Gulf of Mexico. Nearby are the Art Museum of South Texas, the Corpus Christi Museum of Science and History, and the impressive *USS Lexington*.

Whataburger
(1950)

I couldn't resist at least mentioning Whataburger since the first
one opened in my hometown of Corpus Christi. According to
Whataburger Inc.'s official history, Harmon A. Dobson in 1950
sold the first Whataburger from a wooden portable stand mea-
suring 10-by-23 feet. He grilled burgers and hawked cold
drinks and potato chips. In 1953 a Whataburger opened in
Kingsville. That same year the first franchise was awarded to
Joe Andrews in Alice. In 1961 Dobson built a three-story,
A-frame building in Corpus Christi and painted the roof with
alternating orange-and-white stripes. By 1972 the company
had expanded to 100 locations. Since then Whataburger Inc.,
still headquartered in Corpus, has grown to more than 500 restaurants in eight states and the country of Mexico.

Then and now, a Whataburger burger starts with a grilled
quarter-pound patty of 100 percent beef, served on a 5-inch
bun. Depending on a customer's order, staff then pile on lettuce, three tomato slices, four dill pickle slices, and chopped
onions. The bread is spread with mustard, salad dressing, or
ketchup, again depending on the customer's specifications.

Within the last two decades, Whataburger's menu has
greatly expanded to include breakfast (taquitos, biscuits, cinnamon rolls, muffins, and more), beef and chicken fajitas,
chicken strips and sandwiches, fish sandwiches, and salads.
But my husband Terry's all-time favorite is still the classic
Whataburger. Another Corpus native, he remembers a
Whataburger restaurant on Gollihar Road with a steep A-line
roof and covered parking out front. He and his three siblings
ordered many a burger there as kids.

Falls City

Shorty's Place
(about 1946)

A few miles south of a small town called Falls City is Shorty's Place, which sits atop a rise in the highway across from the railroad tracks. The tracks are long gone and grown over with weeds, but Shorty's survives.

Shorty and Ma McGill opened the roadside eatery around 1946. A black-and-white photo of the couple on the wall shows a scraggly bearded man in a cowboy hat and vest standing next to a stout woman wearing a long skirt and bonnet. In another old-timey portrait taken in 1954, Shorty, clad in his scruffy Western attire and pointing an index finger at the camera, poses next to two large wagon wheels.

Like its namesake, Shorty's ain't fancy. Nothing's put on or made up for looks here. Everything's authentic, down to the weathered pine planks laid diagonally on the floor and the dark-brown paneling covering the walls. A collection of 30-odd antlers, all mounted on individual plaques, hang high up on two walls, and a strand of tiny Christmas lights loops from one to the next. OK, the yellow chairs made of molded plastic and the school-cafeteria tables aren't original to the cafe, but the two wooden booths, the counter, and the mirrored bar in back sure are. So is the old wooden telephone booth with its folding glass door. "When the telephone company took out the phone, they wanted to take the booth, too," recalled a long-time cook. "But Ms. Lillian told 'em 'No, we paid for everything when we bought this place.' "

"Yeah, we did everything we could to keep it," says present owner Lillian Beam. "It's part of the place."

Back when Shorty and Ma ran the cafe, they raised everything they served in the backyard, like chicken, squabs, and rabbits. Then health regulations came along and ended that, Lillian says. Fried rabbit is still on the menu, and customers from near and far keep coming to dine at Shorty's. "People drive from San Antonio and Corpus to eat with us," she says. "It's strange, but it happens, and we're grateful. Falls City has only 450 people. If we had to depend on them, we'd starve to death."

Gettin' there: Falls City is just north of Karnes City on U.S. 181. Shorty's is a few miles south of town.

Shorty's Place
Highway 181 S.
Falls City, TX 78113
830/254-3322

The Beam family also runs two other Shorty's restaurants:

Shorty's Place
702 S. Washington St.
Beeville, TX 78102
361/358-7302

Shorty's Place III
4410 E. Highway 97
Pleasanton, TX 78064
830/569-3596

Helotes

Grey Moss Inn
(1929)

Old-time restaurants, vintage buildings, restless spirits, unexplained happenings. Somewhere in this book, we just had to run into a few ghosts, right? Well, we found some at the venerable Grey Moss Inn north of San Antonio.

Nell Baeten, who's owned the restaurant since 1987, has encountered several spirits, both friendly and cranky. She believes one to be the spirit of Mary Howell, who opened the inn in 1929 and died during the fifties. At times, Nell says, Howell becomes frustrated and throws large metal pots on the kitchen floor early in the morning, a ruckus that sets off alarms and perplexes employees. At times the spirit even overturns wine buckets and breaks glasses while customers are eating. Several years ago, when a new computer refused to work, Nell had a stern talk with the spirit. A few minutes later the computer worked.

Nell also believes the spirit of a weeping woman drifts through an area between the inn's herb garden and an underground spring. And once a fire broke out in one of the dining rooms, set—she theorizes—by an unfriendly ghost.

Whatever triggers the strange occurrences, they sure don't deter folks from driving out of their way to eat at the quaint Grey Moss Inn, built of rock beneath a canopy of ancient live oaks. Back when, according to the menu, Mary sold candy from her front porch and cooked up her famous cumin-herbed squash casserole—still served to this day—from squash grown in her garden. When World War II caused a beef shortage, Mary cooked cabrito (goat meat) on an old mesquite grill, and the customers kept coming.

These days Nell and her husband, Lou, are perpetuating the inn's reputation for fine dining and warm atmosphere. They also serve many of the recipes made famous by Mary, such as the aforementioned squash casserole and her popular olive twists. At the inn, every meal starts with a small basket of the rolls—bread sticks specked with bits of black olives. Next, a round of appetizers could include a shrimp cocktail, Grey Moss oysters (rolled in herbed bread crumbs and sauteed), wild game sausage, or fresh mushrooms sauteed in garlic, herbs, and wine. Entrees come with squash au gratin and sour cream potatoes on the half shell. Grilled steaks, smoked chicken, grilled lobster tail and snapper, lamb chops with fresh rosemary Cabernet sauce, and even a vegetarian special (seasonal fresh vegetables served with a broiled tomato, squash au gratin, and a sour cream potato on the half shell) appeal to most diets and taste buds. An extensive wine list and tempting dessert menu rounds out an evening at the inn.

Though prices aren't inexpensive, the restaurant's cozy ambiance makes the time and money spent well worth the drive. And who knows . . . perhaps one of Nell's friendly spirits might pop in for a visit while you're there.

You never know.

Gettin' there: The Grey Moss Inn is located north of San Antonio off Loop 1604 on Scenic Loop Road between Helotes and Leon Springs.

Grey Moss Inn
P.O. 734
19010 Scenic Loop Rd.
Helotes, TX 78023
210/695-8301

Jalapeño Potatoes
25-28 GMI twice-baked potatoes (one tray)
1 18-inch tray of crisply baked bacon
15 whole pickled jalapeños
2 large white onions, finely chopped
$\frac{1}{4}$ cup melted unsalted butter
8 ounces grated cheddar cheese
8 ounces grated mozzarella cheese

Saute onions in butter until tender. Chop jalapeños and bacon. Mix cheeses together.

Cut off the top halves of the GMI potatoes. Distribute onions, jalapeños, bacon, and cheeses equally over the potatoes, which are still in the shells. Replace top half of the potatoes and mold potatoes together at the seams. Brush with melted butter and sprinkle with paprika. Heat at 350 degrees to serving temperature.

Grey Moss Inn Potatoes on the Half-Shell
4 large baking potatoes

Wash and dry potatoes. Grease lightly and bake until tender. Cut in half lengthwise and carefully scoop the potato meat into a mixing bowl. Leave some of the potato (approximately $\frac{1}{4}$ inch) on the skin for a sturdy boat. Reserve these "boats" for filling.

Add to the mixing bowl:
1 egg
1 teaspoon salt
$\frac{1}{4}$ teaspoon black pepper
$\frac{1}{2}$ cup warmed milk
4 tablespoons melted butter
$\frac{1}{2}$ cup sour cream
1 tablespoon chives or green onion tops

Mix all ingredients, except chives, thoroughly. Whip until the mixture is smooth. Stir in chives. Fill "boats" with mixture and sprinkle with paprika. Bake 20 minutes at 350 degrees.

Variations: Add $\frac{1}{2}$ cup grated cheese or $\frac{1}{2}$ cup crisply fried bacon morsels after the mixture has been whipped. Can also top with grated cheese before baking. Yields 8 servings.

Squash Au Gratin

Wash four or five medium zucchini. Slice thinly and steam until tender.

Saute in butter:
1 medium onion, diced
1 small green pepper, diced

Add:
2 tablespoons tomato paste
$\frac{1}{2}$ teaspoon cumin
salt and pepper to taste
dash of Tabasco

Cook on low heat for five minutes and set aside. Drain and mash zucchini. Add onion and tomato paste mixture. Put in a shallow casserole dish.

Grate $\frac{1}{2}$ cup of yellow cheese. Spread over the casserole. Top with $\frac{1}{2}$ cup dry bread crumbs. Dot with butter and bake at 325 degrees for 20 minutes or until slightly brown. Serve in squares.

Chocolate Pecan Pie

1 4-ounce package Bakers German Sweet Chocolate
2 tablespoons margarine or butter
1 cup corn syrup

⅓ cup sugar
3 eggs
1 teaspoon vanilla
1 ½ cups pecan halves
1 unbaked 9-inch pie shell

Preheat oven to 350 degrees. Microwave chocolate and margarine in large microwaveable bowl at High 2 minutes or until margarine is melted. Stir until chocolate is completely melted. Mix in corn syrup, sugar, eggs, and vanilla until well blended. Stir in pecans. Reserve eight for garnish, if desired. Bake one hour or until knife inserted 1 inch from center comes out clean. Cool on wire rack. Garnish with whipped topping and pecan halves, if desired. Makes 8 servings.

Grey Moss Inn French Apple Pie

Spray a 9-inch pie pan with Pam. Line pan with piecrust. Peel and thinly slice 1 pound of apples (approximately five). Place in a large bowl. Sprinkle 2 tablespoons lemon juice over them and stir gently.

Add:
½ cup chopped pecans
¼ cup golden raisins that have soaked in rum

Mix in a small bowl:
½ cup brown sugar
½ cup white sugar
½ teaspoon cinnamon
⅛ teaspoon nutmeg
2 tablespoons flour

Pour spice mixture over apples. Stir gently. Pour apples into pie pan. Dot with butter. Roll out top crust and place over apples. Slice small vent slits in top crust. Brush crust lightly with cream and dust lightly with sugar. Bake at 350 degrees for 45 minutes to an hour or until crust is golden.

Hondo

Hermann Sons Steak House
(1946)

Alvin Britsch started in the restaurant business in 1937 when
he opened the Bobcat Grill in Hondo. For a while he quit the
business. He returned to it, though, in 1946 when he and his
son, Leroy Horace, joined six men from the Hermann Sons
Lodge and moved some barracks from the Hondo air base to
the present location.

In the beginning at his new restaurant, Alvin planned to
serve only a limited menu that included hamburgers and
homemade chili. One day, however, a salesman walked in carrying a brown bag. Inside was a steak, which the man asked
Alvin to prepare. The customer enjoyed his meal so much that
he suggested Alvin add steaks to the menu. Alvin did, and,
well, you can guess the rest of the story.

In the years since, Alvin's son and daughter-in-law, Leroy and Grace, owned and operated the restaurant. In 1994 the couple retired and passed the business to their son, Bryce Britsch.

The steak house's "Pepper Steaks" have been a tradition since Alvin created it in 1939. The 100-percent-pure beef patties are stuffed with onions, cheese, and hot peppers, then seasoned hot, medium hot, or mild. Naturally, Hermann Sons also serves sirloins, filet mignons, T-bones, and chicken-fried steaks (there's a Mexican version of the latter topped with salsa and cheese). Shrimp, oysters, fish, enchiladas, and sandwiches are also served. Homemade peach cobbler or a slice of pie nicely rounds out a meal at Hermann Sons Steak House.

Gettin' there: Hondo is located 40 miles west of San Antonio on U.S. 90.

Hermann Sons Steak House
E. Highway 90
Hondo, TX 78861
830/426-2220

Kenedy

Barth's Restaurant
(about 1936)

When you're a kid, eating at the same ol' place time after time gets to be BOR-RING. Back in the sixties, every time we drove to San Marcos from Corpus Christi to visit my grandparents, we'd stop at Barth's Restaurant in Kenedy. "Not again!" I'd whine as Dad turned into the parking lot. This time, though, some three decades later, I couldn't wait to visit Barth's so I could compare the snapshot memories from my childhood to the restaurant of today.

"The lollipop tree!" I exclaimed as my husband and I pulled up to the restaurant. "Oh, my goodness! I'd forgotten about the lollipop tree. It's still here!"

The lollipop tree, as my brother, Steven, and I called it, stands just inside the glass doors at Barth's. The "limbs" are four poles strung crossways to the "trunk," another pole embedded in a pot of concrete. The suckers are stuck in holes drilled into the tree's limbs. A sign at the tree's top reads, "12 or under, 1 free sucker. Only exception—112 years or older with birth certificate and accompanied by parents." When Barth's changed hands several years ago, the lollipop tree went with it. "It was in pretty sad shape," says the manager with a shrug. "So we repainted it."

Not much else has changed at Barth's either. I remember sitting in the big, circular booth in the corner, watching people perch on twirling stools at the front counter. I also kept an eye on the old wooden telephone booth, built right into the wall. Yes, it's still there, too. Out front, a covered carport shades customers' vehicles while they're eating, just as it has for decades. And the menu still offers the range of food it always did: chicken-fried steak, steaks and shrimp, burgers, chef salads, and even Mexican food. And yes, they still serve baskets of freshly baked homemade bread.

I remember THAT very well, too.

Gettin' there: Kenedy is located approximately 60 miles southeast of San Antonio on U.S. 181.

Barth's Restaurant
445 N. Sunset Strip
Kenedy, TX 78119
830/583-2468

La Grange

Bon Ton Restaurant
(1929)

The Bon Ton has been around so long that if you mention the name to a native Texan, he or she will instantly know you've been through La Grange. Even though it's changed locations a few times, the Bon Ton has held onto its well-known reputation for good down-home cooking, not to mention those famous kolaches and crusty loaves of homemade bread.

And now for the rest of the story... L.D. Weikel in 1929 opened the first Bon Ton location near downtown. The cafe had a long counter along one side and six tables on the other. His first employees were a French cook and one waitress. At the end of the first day, everyone realized the restaurant didn't have a name. So the cook, who evidently had had a lot of fun over the stove that day, suggested "Bon Ton," which means "good time" in French.

Several years later the restaurant moved up the street next door to the Lester Hotel. Salesmen traveling by train got off at the nearby depot, dined at the Bon Ton, and stayed overnight at the hotel. During this era, L.D.'s brother, Alvin, joined the business. At the restaurant, Alvin worked with a charming young waitress named Anita whom he married in 1936.

In the late forties L.D. died, and Alvin took over. In 1972 he sold the restaurant to his only son, Jim, who moved it to Highway 71 in hopes of attracting more customers from passing traffic. To lure them, Jim initiated buffet-style meals, a tradition continued to this day. In 1981 he sold the Bon Ton to new owners, who again moved the restaurant, this time to its present location on the Highway 71 West bypass. The restaurant closed briefly in 1997 but reopened the following year when the Weikel family bought it back.

Today, Jill Stueber, a fourth-generation Weikel, owns the Bon Ton. "I got it by default," she jokes. "I'm the only grandchild who had worked in the kitchen with our grandmother Anita. We have third, fourth, and fifth generation Weikels working here. My uncle makes the kolaches and sells them next door at the convenience store, and my sister Jackie is still baking her famous bread."

Seven days a week, the Bon Ton serves a buffet-style lunch with lots of salads, meats, vegetables, and fresh bread. Evening buffets are served Friday, Saturday, and Sunday. The Saturday and Sunday morning buffets attract folks by the droves. Customers who'd rather order off the menu can choose from a variety of fare, such as fried chicken (which, by the way, received an honorable mention from *Texas Monthly* magazine in '99), chicken-fried steak, steaks, fried shrimp and catfish, hamburgers, and sandwiches. "Healthy" selections include a fat-free raspberry marinated grilled chicken breast, grilled or poached salmon, steamed shrimp, and a vegetarian "Gardenburger."

In a special dining room, Jill started her own tradition called the Bistro. Down-home dining at the Bon Ton turns swanky on Thursday, Friday, and Saturday nights. By candlelight, customers can savor such Epicurean delights as pork loin topped with a sage and balsamic vinegar sauce; charcoal grilled shrimp marinated in cilantro, garlic, and lime; and grilled rainbow trout with shallots, mushrooms, fresh spinach, and tarragon.

Out front in the parking lot, the restaurant's familiar old sign stands tall. Long-time Texans will recognize that as a bit of Lone Star history, too. It's been beckoning motorists to come eat at the Bon Ton in La Grange for more than 25 years.

Gettin' there: The Bon Ton is located on the west side of La Grange on Texas Business 71 West.

Bon Ton Restaurant
2359 W. State Hwy. 71
P.O. Box 624
La Grange, TX 78945
409/968-8875

Stop by and see: Take a lovely stroll beneath the towering live oaks at Monument Hill State Historic Site, the final resting place of the men who drew black beans of death after the 1842 Mier Expedition against Mexico. Victims of the 1842 Dawson Massacre are entombed here, too. Bonus: You can also tour the Kreische Brewery State Historic Site, located adjacent to Monument Hill.

Five-cup Salad
1 16-ounce can pineapple chunks
1 banana, sliced
1 11-ounce can mandarin oranges, drained
1 cup miniature marshmallows
½ cup coconut
1 cup sour cream

Mix, chill, and serve.

"We serve this squash casserole on our buffet line, and people just die for it," Jill says.

Baked Squash Casserole

2 pounds frozen yellow squash
3 cups cracker crumbs
3 eggs
1 ½ cups milk
1 ½ cups processed cheese, shredded
¼ cup margarine, softened
⅓ cup chopped onion
1 pound hamburger meat, lean, cooked and drained
salt, pepper

Beat eggs, milk, and margarine together. Steam squash; mix with cracker crumbs and cooked meat. Season to taste. Add egg mixture. Mix well. If stiff, add more milk. Add cheese to mixture, stir. Spray baking pan with Pam. Fill two-thirds full. Bake approximately 20 minutes at 350 degrees. Top with shredded cheese, if desired.

Oatmeal Pies

(makes 4)
8 eggs
2 cups sugar
4 cups white Karo syrup
2 cups butter, melted
4 teaspoons vanilla
2 cups coconut
2 cups pecan pieces
4 cups oatmeal

Mix together. Pour into four unbaked, 9-inch deep-dish pie shells. Bake at 350 degrees for 45 minutes to an hour, or until moderately firm. (Recipe can easily be divided to make one pie.)

Update: As of publication date, Bon Ton was closed for business and doubtful to reopen. Make sure to call before visiting this establishment. The recipes are still great.

Lake Jackson

Harnden's Dairy Bar
(1956)

For more than four decades, Harnden's Dairy Bar has been a popular teenage hangout. It started back in the fifties when Ernest "Slim" Harnden, a Yokum native, visited a friend in Bay City and was impressed with the man's hamburger stand.

"So I thought I would check out the area for a location for me to start something like that," Harnden reminisced in a 1990 issue of the *Brazosport Facts*. "As I was headed south, I saw a sign saying 'Lake Jackson.' Well, I had my fishing pole with me so I decided to do some fishing at the lake. I never did find the lake that day, but I did find a little drive-in for sale."

He and his wife, Dorothy, bought Deville's Drive-in on Plantation Drive, which back then was a two-lane, blacktop road. The couple flipped hamburgers and whirled up milkshakes and malts. Six years later, the Harndens outgrew the drive-in and built a bigger one on Plantation Drive.

After all these years, Harnden's Dairy Bar still serves a lot of burgers from fresh-ground meat (more than 600 pounds a week), raised and processed on the family's ranch. "We're best known in the area for our jalapeño burgers," says daughter, Mary Harnden. "They're made of two hamburger patties with jalapeños and cheese in the middle. They're wonderful"

In fact, almost everything but the fries are made from scratch, including the ice cream (served in the delectable form of cones, banana splits, sundaes, malts, and shakes) and onion rings. The drive-in also serves sandwiches, "basket" meals (like steak fingers, catfish, and chicken tenders), salads, hot dogs, Frito pie, and nachos.

Gettin' there: From Texas 332, turn east on Plantation Drive. Harnden's Dairy Bar is on the north side of the street between Garland Drive and Sycamore Street.

Harnden's Dairy Bar
202 Plantation Dr.
Lake Jackson, TX 77566
409/297-3256

Stop by and see: The nearby Sea Center Texas is a $13 million facility that features saltwater aquariums, exhibits, outdoor marshes, and the world's largest red drum (redfish) hatchery in the world.

Laredo

La Mexicana Restaurant
(1954)

Crisp flautas—corn tortillas filled with chicken or beef, rolled up and lightly fried—rank high on my list of favorite Mexican foods. La Mexicana Restaurant prides itself on serving the tastiest ones in Laredo.

Jose Magdaleno Lailson and his wife, Bertha, in 1927 opened Loncheria La Mexicana in Torreon, Coahuila, Mexico. A decade later they moved to Nuevo Laredo and opened La Mexicana, serving tacos and flautas. In 1954 they moved again, this time across the border to San Bernardo Avenue in Laredo. The restaurant served the first flautas in town. At one time, two La Mexicanas operated on the busy thoroughfare. In 1987 the restaurant moved to its present location at the intersection of Santa Ursula and Sanchez, right off the interstate.

In 1967 Lailson died, but Bertha kept the business going. She still works there. These days her granddaughter, Sylvia Whitlock, manages the busy restaurant.

The restaurant's popular flautas are served crisp or soft, plain or topped with a spicy sauce of seasoned stewed onions, tomatoes, and sweet peppers. Besides flautas, La Mexicana serves a variety of other Mexican specialties, such as beef tripe stew, tostadas, enchiladas, and mole. For dessert, there's Mexican-style vanilla custard with caramel sauce.

Gettin' there: South on I-35, exit Park Street and stay on southbound access road (Santa Ursula Avenue). La Mexicana Restaurant sits at the corner of Santa Ursula and Sanchez Street.

La Mexicana Restaurant
1902 Santa Ursula Ave.
Laredo, TX 78040
956/723-4641

Stop by and see: A mere 35 cents will get you across the International Bridge to Guerrero Street in Nuevo Laredo, a shopping mecca of bargains. Return toll to get back into Laredo is a quarter. Remember, don't drink the water unless it's bottled.

Chicken Flautas
whole fryer
salt
oil
corn tortillas

81

Fill a pot with water. Bring to a boil. Add chicken. When cooked, shred the chicken and add salt to taste. Grab a tortilla, fill with chicken and roll up. Fry in hot oil.

▪▪▪▪▪▪▪▪▪▪▪▪▪▪▪▪▪▪▪▪▪▪▪

Rio Grande City

Caro's Restaurant
(1937)

Juan Caro and his wife, Carmen, are busy folks. Caro's Restaurant is the reason why. For more than 60 years, the family-owned institution has served up the finest Tex-Mex cuisine in the region. A big draw is the restaurant's specialty—puffy corn tacos and tostados, made from corn masa. The crisply fried delicacies were created by his mother, Modesta Caro, the original owner of Caro's.

The restaurant business is all Juan's ever known. "I started working in this restaurant when I was six years old," he says. "I helped my mother. She used to bake cakes, and I washed the pans." Juan continued to work there as a teenager. As a young man, he attended Wisconsin University; then he joined the Army. "I was a cook in France," he says. After finishing his service, Juan settled in Fort Worth and in 1952 opened a second Caro's on Blue Bonnet Circle, not far from Texas Christian University. In 1968 Modesta passed away, so Juan returned home to run her cafe. His sister, Lourdes Whitten, runs the Fort Worth location.

On the menu, the closest thing you'll find to "Americanized" fare is a chicken-fried steak (served with French fries) or a T-bone steak. Even then, the T-bone is served with Juan's charra beans, guacamole, rice, tostados, and tortillas. The rest is authentic Tex-Mex fixin's, like enchiladas, tacos, chalupas, and envueltos. Envueltos? What's that, I had to ask Juan. "Beef enchiladas with no cheese, and lettuce and tomatoes," he replies. "They're only made in South Texas."

Throughout its 60-plus years of business, Caro's in Rio Grande City has fed a lot of people including some famous ones. "We've had quite a few governors who have eaten with us, like Governors (Mark) White and (Allan) Shrivers," Juan recalls. "We fed President Johnson once, but not in the restaurant. And President Kennedy came here once, too."

Gettin' there: Caro's is located half a block west of Highway 83, across the street from Ramirez Ford dealership.

Caro's Restaurant
205 N. Garcia St.
Rio Grande City, TX 78582
956/487-2255

Fort Worth location:
3505 Blue Bonnet Cir.
Fort Worth, TX 76109
817/924-9977

Stop by and see: Stop and see the Our Lady of Lourdes Grotto at 305 N. Britton near the Starr County courthouse. The grotto is a replica of the famous shrine in Lourdes, France.

Juan's Charra Beans
1 bag pinto beans
chopped onion
chopped tomato
bacon ends
cilantro
a little bit of oregano
salt, pepper

Wash the beans and place them in a pot. Cover with water and let soak overnight. The next day, cook over low heat approximately 3 hours. Fry some bacon ends with the onion, tomato, cilantro, and oregano. Put in electric blender and swirl around a few times. Then add to beans. Cook another half hour. Taste, add more salt if needed. "When beans are soft, they're ready," Juan Caro says.

Riviera

King's Inn
(1945)

What I remember most about visiting King's Inn as a child was the GETTING THERE. It seemed to take forever. We lived in northwest Corpus Christi, nearly 60 miles away, a huge road trip for a nine-year-old. As we drove along the country road to the restaurant one evening, we passed fields and fields filled with fat watermelons, a heavenly sight for a kid. After eating our fill of seafood at King's Inn, we headed home at dusk and ran out of gas along that same little road. We pulled up to a farm, but no one was home. Daddy spotted some gasoline, poured what was left into our station wagon, and dropped some coins inside a big glass bottle (back then gas was cheap). The little bit of gasoline got us back onto the highway. We made it several miles before we ran out of gas again and had to pull over. Daddy, I think, thumbed his way to a gas station. My memory fogs there, but he must have made it back safely to our car or else I wouldn't be here to tell you this story.

The point is, thousands of faithful patrons gladly go the extra miles to eat at King's Inn. Each year, they devour more than 35,000 pounds of fried jumbo shrimp, the most popular item on the menu. Close behind run fried oysters and fried fish, all caught fresh in the Gulf of Mexico and served family style.

King's Inn originally opened as 1935 as Orlando's Cafe. Blanche Wright later leased and bought the business and renamed it Wright's Cafe. At her death in 1945, she left the cafe to her friends Faye and Cottle Ware. The couple—for the last time—renamed the cafe, which began the King's Inn legacy. Today, the Wares' son and daughter-in-law, Randy and Rhonda Ware, own and operate the restaurant, known far and wide for its delicious seafood.

Gettin' there: From Kingsville, head south on U.S. 77 about 11 miles. Turn east on FM 628 and go about 9 miles. King's Inn is located in the small community of Loyola Beach.

King's Inn
Rt. I Box 58-B
Riviera, TX 78379
361/297-5265

Stop by and see: Ever heard of the King Ranch? Head over to downtown Kingsville and check out the King Ranch Museum, housed in a restored ice plant at 405 N. Sixth St. Exhibits tell the story of the 825,000-acre enterprise, established in 1853 by Capt. Richard King when he bought 75,000 acres that had been a Spanish land grant called Santa Gertrudis.

Rockport

Duck Inn Restaurant
(1946)

From the windows at the Duck Inn, you can see the Rockport beach and the big pink scalloped shell that faces the inland. I remember sitting at a table as a child, peering at that huge seashell. It's still big. The same neon sign with a duck flapping its wings (when lit) still stands next to the restaurant. It's been there ever since I was a kid. And probably a bit longer than that, too.

Charlie Duck opened Duck Inn in 1946. "He ran the front of the restaurant, and his wife cooked," explains Burt Mills, who now owns the popular restaurant. "My wife and I run it the same way he did. I take care of the front, and she runs the kitchen."

The Duck Inn specializes in fresh seafood. So fresh, the menu proclaims, that "the fish you order today, last night could have slept in the bay!"

Can't decide what to get? Then choose the "special seafood platter," and you'll get a bit of everything—shrimp cocktail, fried fish and shrimp, stuffed crab, an oyster and scallop, a crab claw, and shrimp salad. Of course, you can order a regular plate of whatever you fancy, like broiled shrimp or fried flounder. The Duck also serves steaks, chicken-fried steak, fried chicken, burgers, and BLTs.

Gettin' there: The Duck Inn is located on Texas 35 across from Rockport Beach.

Duck Inn
701 Highway 35 N.
Rockport, TX 78382
361/729-6663

Stop by and see: The Texas Maritime Museum (on Texas 35 near the harbor) honors the state's maritime heritage with exhibits and interactive displays.

Round Top

Royers' Round Top Cafe
(1947)

In Texas's smallest incorporated town, you'd expect to pull up a chair at the local cafe, watch the old-timers chug coffee at the next table, and order yourself a burger wrapped in wax paper and served in a plastic basket.

Not gonna happen at Royers' in Round Top (population 81).

For one thing, an empty table at this wildly popular cafe is hard to get (expect at least a two-hour wait during weekends).

And for another, Royers' serves artfully prepared, citified cooking, not the down-home fare dished out at a typical country cafe.

The cafe's been around since 1947, but the Royers didn't become a part of it until four decades later. Bud Royers and his wife, Karen, were living and working in Houston when the local economy went bust in the mid-eighties, and Bud lost his job as a restaurant consultant. To help make ends meet and feed their four children, Karen taught piano lessons. In April 1987 some friends in Round Top called and offered to sell their cafe to the Royers, who had visited the community often in the past. "There was no way we could buy the cafe—we couldn't even buy groceries," writes Karen in the family's cookbook, *The Royers' Round Top Cafe: A Relational Odyssey*. They couldn't afford gasoline either. But determined and committed to following up every possible job lead, the family borrowed some money, gassed up the car, and headed for Round Top. Within weeks, they owned the Round Top Cafe.

Though anxious to add their own touches to the restaurant, the Royers made the menu their top priority. First to go was the barbecue. In its place came chicken fingers with honey mustard. They also beefed-up dessert selections and started serving pies, bread puddings, and strawberry shortcake. Bud's chocolate chip pie quickly generated a devoted following as did the cafe's other pies. The menu changes worked, and the little restaurant's 38 seats filled up regularly.

All the Royers' hard work, though, barely paid their bills. So, encouraged by their clientele (most of whom were from Houston and very well off), Bud and Karen upped their prices and expanded the menu even more, adding such sophisticated bistro-style foods as fresh pastas and salmon, grilled quail, and marinated pork ribs. It wasn't long before lines began to form for tables on the weekends.

More than a decade later, the Royers have kept to their upscale cooking. On the cafe's hand-lettered, chatty menu, you'll find all sorts of intriguing dishes, such as Mexican pasta (fettucine topped with salsa, grilled onions, tomatoes, cheese, guacamole, and sour cream), grilled red snapper, "Funky Bleu Chest" (a chicken breast topped with grilled onions and bleu cheese dressing), and a "Monster Pork Chop" (a 12-ounce, center-cut chop grilled and topped with grilled onions with red-raspberry chipotle sauce on the side).

And the pies . . . they're so popular that Bud ships them as part of the family's mail-order business. Besides his famous chocolate chip Tollhouse, the cafe serves cherry, apple, peach, blueberry, pecan, buttermilk, and butterscotch Tollhouse. All slices come with a scoop of vanilla ice cream. Bud actually charges two bits extra if you DON'T want ice cream with your pie. "We are thinking about charging you for pie even if you don't have any," the menu jokes. "Why come all this way and not have our pie?!?!?!"

Gettin' there: Round Top is located on Texas 237 midway between Brenham and La Grange.

Royers' Round Top Cafe
P.O. Box 207
Round Top, Texas 78954
409/249-3611
877/866-7437
Website: www.royerscafe.com

Stop by and see: If you love antiques, plan to visit Round Top during the first weekend in April or October (or both!). That's when the Round Top Antique Fair brings thousands of shoppers to this tiny little town of 81 people.

The following recipes are excerpts from the family's 175-page cookbook *Royers' Round Top Cafe: A Relational Odyssey*. Copies of the hard-bound book, Bud's famous pies, and other merchandise can be ordered from the Royers' toll-free number.

The Cafe's Jalapeño Cheese Soup

¼ pound butter
1 teaspoon baking soda
¾ cup flour
6 tablespoons cornstarch
1½ quarts water
16 chicken bouillon cubes, crushed
2 tablespoons minced canned jalapeños
6 cups milk
16 ounces sliced American cheese
1 medium onion, chopped
½ stalk celery, chopped
½ cup chopped carrots

To make roux, melt butter in a skillet. Add baking soda, flour, and cornstarch. Mix together until it thickens. In a 10-quart stock pot, bring the water, crushed chicken bouillon cubes, and the jalapeños to a boil. Add the roux to the boiling water, and stir until the roux thickens and begins to boil. Add the milk to the boiling mixture and stir until the milk is completely mixed into the mixture. Turn the heat down to medium-low. Add the cheese a slice at a time and continue to stir until the cheese is completely melted. Add the vegetables to the soup and turn off the burner. This soup is not "hot," but it is very flavorful! It will hold in the refrigerator for only two days or so. Yield: 1¾ gallons.

Andy's Pasta

16 (1-ounce) skinless, boneless chicken breast strips (if you can't find tenders, just slice 3 to 4 chicken breasts into strips)
½ cup flour
1 cup softened dill butter
¼ cup chopped green onion tops
3 small tomatoes, cut into 12 wedges
4 to 5 medium or large mushrooms, sliced
3 cups Andy's Pasta Sauce (recipe follows)
12 ounces egg fettuccine
½ cup melted butter
1 cup grated Parmesan cheese
chopped parsley for garnish

Lightly bread the chicken strips in flour. In a large skillet, heat the dill butter and saute the chicken strips until lightly browned. Add to skillet the green onions, tomatoes, and mushrooms, and cook for 2 minutes so that the vegetables are seasoned with the dill butter. Add Andy's Pasta Sauce to the mixture and heat for a minute or so until the sauce is hot. If the sauce is too thin, add Parmesan cheese to thicken it. If it is too thick, add white wine to thin it. You will want the sauce thick enough to hold to the pasta.

Cook the fettuccine al dente, drain, and mix in ½ cup melted butter and ½ cup of the grated Parmesan cheese. Divide the pasta between four plates. Place four chicken strips on top of each plate of pasta along with three tomato wedges. Spoon vegetables and sauce onto each plate. Sprinkle the remaining grated Parmesan cheese on top and garnish with chopped parsley. Yield: 4 servings.

Andy's Pasta Sauce

½ cup margarine
⅓ cup (or more) flour
1 quart milk
½ (750-ml) bottle inexpensive white wine
½ quart heavy whipping cream
1 ounce Worcestershire sauce

Melt the margarine in a large saucepan over medium heat. Add the flour, stirring constantly. Add the milk gradually. Cook for 4 minutes. Add the wine, whipping cream, and Worcestershire sauce. Cook for 10 to 12 minutes, stirring constantly. Do not bring to a boil or the mixture will separate. Yield: 4 servings.

Italian Cream Cake

1 cup buttermilk
1 teaspoon baking soda
5 eggs, separated
2 cups sugar
1 stick butter, softened
$\frac{1}{2}$ teaspoon salt
1 cup shortening
2 cups flour
1 teaspoon vanilla extract
1 cup pecans or walnuts
1 cup flaked coconut

Combine the buttermilk and baking soda; let stand for several minutes. Beat egg whites until stiff peaks form. Cream sugar, butter, salt, and shortening until light and fluffy. Add egg yolks, one at a time, beating well after each addition. Add flour and buttermilk a little at a time, mixing well after each addition. Add vanilla, nuts, and coconut. Fold in egg whites gently. Spoon into three greased and floured 9-inch cake pans. Bake at 325 degrees for 25 minutes. Cool in pans for several minutes. Turn onto wire racks to cool completely.

When cool, ice with the following:
1 stick butter, softened
8 ounces cream cheese, softened
1 box confectioners sugar, approximately
1 teaspoon vanilla extract

Cream the butter and cream cheese until fluffy. Add confectioners sugar and vanilla; beat well. Yield: 12 to 16 servings.

Bud's Chocolate Chip Pie

1 cup sugar
1 cup packed brown sugar
1 cup all-purpose flour
2 large eggs, lightly beaten
$\frac{1}{2}$ cup melted, unsalted butter
$\frac{1}{2}$ cup coarsely chopped pecans or walnuts
$\frac{1}{2}$ cup chocolate chips
1 10-inch pie shell, unbaked

Mix sugar, brown sugar, and flour together. Stir in the eggs and then the butter, combining well. Fold in the nuts and chocolate chips. Spread in the prepared crust and bake at 325 degrees for 60 to 70 minutes or until a knife inserted in the center comes out clean. This pie freezes exceptionally well, if it lasts that long! Yields: 8 servings.

San Antonio

Casa Rio
(1946)

Tree-shaded and lush, the River Walk in San Antonio ranks high among tourists' favorite places to visit. Lined with restaurants and clubs, the walkway along the San Antonio River is colorful by day and twinkling at night.

But it wasn't always like that. In the mid-forties people stayed away from the River Walk because of the pickpockets who lurked there after dark. In spite of its bad reputation, the area caught Alfred Beyer's attention. Despite three business failures of his own, Beyer plowed ahead and decided to open a restaurant on the river. Some people thought he was nuts. He didn't care. In 1946 he and his wife, Agnes, built Casa Rio on the site of a Spanish colonial hacienda and incorporated much of the old structure into the new, such as some 18-inch-thick walls, a cedar log door, window lintels, and a fireplace. For many years Casa Rio was the only restaurant on the river.

After opening Casa Rio, Beyer asked the city several times for help in cleaning up the River Walk but was turned down due to lack of funds. Frustrated but undaunted, Beyer set to work himself. Around the restaurant and across the river, he planted trees and elephants ears uprooted from his property on the Comal River. For nighttime appeal, he lit tiki torches on the patio, built a fountain across the river, and hung strands of yellow lights in the trees. He also put up big umbrellas over outside tables so customers could enjoy riverside dining, rain or shine.

Beyer's vision didn't stop there. He also founded the River Walk's river barge tradition, a hugely popular attraction to this day. But the new venture wasn't an easy one to start. Finding the right boat design took time. A heavy gondola sunk. A bridge beheaded a swan boat. An early barge capsized. But by the late sixties river-worthy barges were quietly motoring up and down the river, carrying tourists to see the sights and sometimes feeding them catered meals.

Today, Beyer's grandchildren, Linda Lyons and Bill Lyons run Casa Rio, the oldest restaurant on the River Walk. Like their grandfather did, they still serve the original Regular Plate—a cheese enchilada, a tamale, chili con carne, Mexican rice, and refried beans. Homemade corn tortillas and chili con carne, made from cubed beef simmered with the pulp of ancho chiles, are the restaurant's signature menu items. Though the Mexican food is excellent, visitors surely eat at Casa Rio for the ambiance, riverside dining, and probably their memories of past meals there, too.

Which is exactly what Alfred Beyer wanted to achieve a half century ago.

Gettin' there: From I-37/U.S. 281, exit Commerce Street. Turn west on Commerce. Casa Rio is located at 430 E. Commerce St. on the River Walk. For parking, turn left on Presa Street, then left on Market Street. The Casa Rio parking lot is located on the left. Expect to pay for parking anywhere you go in downtown San Antonio.

Casa Rio
430 E. Commerce St.
San Antonio, TX 78205
210/225-6718

Stop by and see: Underneath the big top of an ornate ceiling, all the thrills and chills of an old-time circus come to life with a visit to the Hertzberg Circus Collection and Museum (210 Market St.), housed in an old library building just a short stroll away from the River Walk.

Casa Rio Green Enchilada Sauce

1 stalk celery, cut into ½-inch pieces
3 large white onions, cut into quarters
3 large bell peppers, sliced and seeds removed
2½ tablespoons ground comino
2½ tablespoons black pepper
1 ounce fresh garlic
¼ cup green onions (optional)
fresh chicken base or ½ pound chicken base paste

Place all ingredients into a 7-quart pot. Add chicken broth and enough water to cover the ingredients. Bring to a boil, letting vegetables cook until tomatoes are done to softness. Remove from stove and place into food processor, blending into a sauce.

Please note: This sauce is to have noticeable chunks of onion, tomato, and celery. Do not keep in the food processor too long!

Earl Abel's
(1952)

A flaky slice of warm apple pie with a scoop of melting vanilla ice cream—that's the mental picture I get when I think of Earl Abel's.

Back in my college days, the Art Deco-style restaurant on Broadway Avenue was the place to take a break when we students pulled all-nighters. On those after-dark escapades, I usually ordered apple pie with the works. Though businesses along Broadway have come and gone in the years since, Earl Abel's remains the same. Thank goodness.

Manager Jerry Abel's father, Earl, opened the restaurant in 1952. His kidney bean-shaped sign still stands at the corner of the parking lot, promising "This is Earl Abel's 24-Hour Restaurant" in neon red-and-green letters. Inside, 'round the clock, waitresses in uniforms and thick-soled shoes still take orders for fried chicken ("it's simply delicious," proclaims the menu), steaks, fish, burgers, tacos, pancakes, eggs, and biscuits, and—of course—cakes and pies.

Speaking of pie, the day's fresh-baked selections of pies (such as coconut meringue, lemon chess, black bottom, and chocolate icebox) still sit in a high, tilted shelf in front of the diner-style counter, where customers can pull up a chair and chow down. Overhead, one of several witty signs reads, "Eating good food keeps you able. Eating here keeps Earl Abel."

Amen.

Gettin' there: Located at the corner of Broadway and Hildebrand, not far from Brackenridge Park and the Witte Museum.

Earl Abel's
4200 Broadway St.
San Antonio, TX 78209
210/822-3358

Stop by and see: Around the corner from Earl Abel's is the San Antonio Zoo in Brackenridge Park. Many of the zoo's 3,000 residents, the third largest collection in North America, wander about in naturalistic, open-air settings. The Witte Museum of History and Science at 3801 Broadway is another must-see.

Jim's Restaurants, Tower of the Americas Restaurant, and Magic Time Machine
(Frontier Enterprises, 1946)

Jim's Restaurants. The Magic Time Machine. And the Tower of Americas. What do those three very different restaurants share in common? One man by the name of Jim Hasslocher.

His story begins after World War II when he returned home to San Antonio in 1946. Eager to start his own business, the young man opened a bicycle stand at the entrance to Brackenridge Park and rented bikes to GIs stationed at nearby bases. When watermelon season arrived, Jim expanded his business and sold slices of ice-cold fruit to the servicemen after they'd enjoyed their bike rides through the park. A year later he joined the post-war burger craze and opened the Frontier Drive-in, complete with cowgirl-attired carhops. The drive-in restaurant became so popular that Jim opened more in town and in Austin, too.

Jim's Restaurants

In 1963 Jim and his wife, Veva, decided to test another trend—coffee shops—and opened Jim's Coffee Shop in the Alamo City. The venture became the forerunner of the successful line of Jim's Restaurants. Today 27 Jim's Restaurants, located in San Antonio, Austin, Temple, Waco, and San Marcos, serve customers 'round the clock. The restaurants' extensive menus include eggs, biscuits, pancakes, burgers, sandwiches, salads, soups, vegetables, chili, seafood, steaks, and great desserts (cobblers, pies, brownie sundaes, milkshakes, and cheesecakes).

Tower Restaurant

Five years later the Hosslochers really set their sights HIGH when they decided to operate the Tower Restaurant located in the Tower of Americas, a 750-foot-tall "needle" built for HemisFair, the 1968 World's Fair. At 550 feet high, the circular restaurant's revolving dining room makes one revolution per hour, offering an awesome view of San Antonio and the surrounding Hill Country. In addition to the magnificent vistas, the Tower Restaurant offers an elegant atmosphere and fine cuisine (steaks, prime rib, heavy aged beef, chicken, and seafood), making it a memorable place to celebrate any special occasion.

Magic Time Machine Restaurant

In 1973 the couple switched gears and opened a restaurant unlike any other restaurant—the Magic Time Machine. Their concept was so unusual that, a year later, they won the

97

International Food Manufacturers Association's coveted Golden Plate Award.

What makes the Magic Time Machine Restaurant so different? Well, customers don't just enjoy a meal out; they EXPERIENCE it. Wait staff dressed like popular personalities escort people to tables tucked away in dark "themed" alcoves, such as a Spanish hide-a-way, a jail cell, mine shaft, and orgy pit. Back in the seventies Tony the Tiger, Daisy Mae, Peter Pan, and Herbie the Cow seated customers and joked the rest of the evening with them. These days Braveheart, Poison Ivy, Ace Ventura, and Catwoman are among the crazy characters that breeze through the restaurant, carrying plates of food and yelling "potty patrol!" whenever a customer innocently asks for directions.

Speaking of food, it hasn't changed much either. The same 1953 MG Roadster, which serves as the salad bar, still keeps the soups hot, the salads chilled, and an ample supply of crispy cheese wafers ready. Grilled seafood and steaks dominate the menu, and the famous "Roman Orgy" still attracts attention whenever folks order one. The huge spread includes roasted chicken, brisket, corn on the cob, carrots, and fresh fruit.

And to think it all started with bikes and watermelons. . . .

Jim's Restaurants
Locations in San Antonio, Austin, San Marcos, Waco, and Temple
Website: www.eat-at-jims.com

Magic Time Machine   Second location:
902 NE Loop 410   5003 Beltline Dr.
San Antonio, TX 78209   Dallas, TX
210/828-1470   972/980-1903
Website: http://magictimemachine.com

Tower of Americas Restaurant
2222 HemisFair Park
San Antonio, TX 78205
210/223-3101
Website: http://toweroftheamericas.com

Stop by and see: Beneath the Tower of Americas is the Institute of Texan Cultures, built in 1968 as the Texas Pavilion at HemisFair. Inside the two-story hall, visitors of all ages can see and experience 27 different cultures found in Texas, all represented within a 50,000-square-foot exhibit area that includes a dome theater and a puppet show. On the 15-acre grounds, replicas of a dog-trot cabin, old schoolhouse, and other early-Texas structures stand beneath the spreading branches of live oaks.

Jim's Restaurants Chicken-Fried Steak

For batter, blend until smooth:
2 quarts Instant Blend
4 cups buttermilk
2 cups water

Per one serving:
1 4-ounce cutlet
1 ounce flour
½ ounce batter

Place cutlet in flour and coat both sides, pressing with palm of hand so that cutlet spreads. Dip cutlet into batter and coat thoroughly. Place cutlet back into flour and coat again, pressing lightly with palm of hand until flour adheres. Place floured cutlet in hot oil (350 degrees) and cook until golden brown. Cutlet will usually float when done. Remove from oil, allow to drain, and blot dry. Serve hot.

Magic Time Machine's Beef Brisket

8- to 9-pound brisket
1 ½ ounces Lawry's seasoned salt
¼ ounce Lawry's seasoned pepper
1 ½ ounces minced dry onions
½ ounce diced dry green bell pepper
¼ ounce Lawry's Pinch of Herbs
¼ ounce paprika
¼ ounce parsley
1 whole bay leaf
browning bag
1 tablespoon flour for bag

Preheat oven to 225 degrees. Trim brisket. With sharp tip of knife, cut eye out of both sides of brisket. Trim fat on top of brisket to about ¼ inch. Season brisket, starting with fat side down and ending with fat side up. Place brisket in bag, shake one tablespoon flour in browning bag, and put one bay leaf on top of brisket. Tie off bag with twisty and place on sheet pan. Puncture four holes with tip of knife in top near twisted closure of bag (keep holes as small as possible to ensure moistness). Bake brisket at 225 degrees for 4-6 hours or until tender. Pull from oven, remove carefully from browning bag. Slice and serve hot.

Tower of the Americas Cheesecake

Crust:
⅓ cup sugar
½ cup melted butter, unsalted
1 cup graham cracker crumbs

Mix all ingredients together. Place mixture into a 9-inch spring-form pan. Chill crust.

Filling:
½ cup chopped pecans
¾ ounces lemon juice
4 tablespoons vanilla extract
½ pound powdered sugar
¾ pound unsalted butter, softened
3 pounds cream cheese, room temperature

Using a Kitchen Aid mixer, whip butter until smooth with the paddle. Add cream cheese and mix thoroughly. Scrape sides of bowl. Add powdered sugar slowly while mixer is on slow speed. Add remaining filling ingredients. Mix until all is incorporated, scraping the sides.

Sauce:
1 package frozen strawberries with sugar

Thaw strawberries; save liquid. Blend in a blender with all the liquid. Keep refrigerated.

Assembling:
When crust is firm, place cream cheese mix on top, smooth out and level. Refrigerate until firm, approximately 4 hours. Remove from spring-form pan and cut with a hot, wet knife. Serve with strawberry sauce. Serves 10.

Mi Tierra Cafe and Bakery
(1941)

The pace at Mi Tierra Cafe and Bakery at the Market Square rarely slows. 'Round the clock, people stream in and out the doors, filling up the 500-plus seats in the dining rooms over and over again. At peak hours, staff feed 400 to 500 people in an hour with as many as 290 more waiting in the bakery and outside the doors for their turn. Meanwhile, waitresses in ruffled blouses and waiters in neatly pressed shirts zip around the tables, carrying huge trays laden with steaming plates of food and jotting down more orders on note pads. Amid the loud din of voices, musicians with guitars stroll from table to table, crooning Mexican melodies for a small fee.

A young Mexican immigrant by the name of Pete Cortez and his beautiful wife, Cruz Llanes, of San Antonio, opened Mi Tierra in 1941. The restaurant fulfilled Pete's long-time dream—to own his own business in America. Proud of his Mexican roots and new American citizenship, he dedicated himself to revitalizing El Mercado (the Market Square) and the Mexican culture that surrounded it. Cortez died in 1984, but he lived long enough to see his second dream come true, too.

Jorge Cortez is one of the couple's five children who run Mi Tierra and two nearby restaurants (La Margarita and Pico de Gallo). Like his father, he's proud of his heritage.

"This place was the produce and farmers' market," he says of the old El Mercado. "It was hustling and rustling all the time. That was why we stayed open 24 hours a day—for the farmers and brokers. When the market moved to another location around '55, it left a vacuum in the area. But my father could see the beauty of what was here and what should be preserved for future generations. He believed it was important not to lose the hub of our community and the energy. Mi Tierra kept the area going because of the many people who came into the restaurant."

Pete Cortez would be both proud and awed by the Mi Tierra he founded nearly six decades ago. Besides serving quality Mexican food to thousands of folks, the local landmark employs 350 people. Once they're hired, many stay, sometimes for generations. "A lot of families work here, like fathers and their children," says Jorge's daughter, Christina Cortez.

Many customers have a way of hanging around for years, too. Literally. High on one wall in the restaurant hang dozens of black-and-white photographs of men's faces. Some are familiar. Most are not. Some are wizened. Many wear horn-rimmed glasses. Their expressions range from pensive to grinning. "We call that the Snake Pit," Jorge explained. "In all great cafes, there's always a group of men who gather there. They are CEOs, presidents of banks, and other men who get together and shoot the bull. I felt honored that they come here so I gave them this wall."

In all, more than 350 other photographs hang throughout Mi Tierra. They commemorate the Cortez family (past and present), community people, historic buildings, and important events in San Antonio. "There's a lot of history here," Jorge reflects. "It's the American story of an immigrant who came in, was blessed by God, and worked very hard. What's made Mi Tierra last these years is the love we instill into everything. That love comes from our pride of our city and our community.

"Mi Tierra is a world-class cafe. It has something to offer to the world."

Gettin' there: Market Square is bounded by Interstate 35, Santa Rosa, Dolorosa, and Commerce Streets, west of downtown.

Mi Tierra Cafe and Bakery
218 Produce Row
San Antonio, TX 78207
210/225-1262

Stop by and see: Stroll across the plaza and browse through El Mercado, a large indoor shopping area patterned after a real Mexican market. More restaurants and shops line the plaza outside El Mercado and inside the Farmers Market Plaza, a recently renovated area of Market Square.

Schilo's
(1917)

A beef tongue sandwich on rye bread? Braunschweiger with crackers? Welcome to Schilo's (pronounced "she-lows"), one of the few places left in San Antonio where you can still get such delicacies.

Fritz Schilo, a German immigrant who moved to Texas in the late 1800s, opened a saloon in Beeville after the turn of the century. In 1914 he moved his family and business to San Antonio on Commerce Street. Prohibition shut down the saloon in 1917. But Fritz wasn't down and out for long. Within a few months he opened a lunchroom on South Alamo Street. In 1927 the restaurant moved to Commerce Street, next door to its present location. With typical German tenacity, the Schilos survived the Depression. After Fritz died in 1935, his son, Edgar, ran the business. In 1942 Schilo's moved to 424 E. Commerce St. and was operated by the family's third generation. Today, Bill Lyons, whose family started Casa Rio on the River Walk, owns and operates Schilo's.

Morning meals at Schilo's are a hearty affair. The "Papa Fritz Breakfast" comes with two eggs, bratwurst, hash browns or grits, toast, biscuits, or muffins, and coffee, milk, or juice. Potato pancakes, "light" pancakes, and French toast come a la carte or with your choice of ham, bacon, sausage, and/or eggs. There's also a tempting selection of bakery goods, like homemade cinnamon rolls, apple or peach streusel, and biscuits with sausage gravy.

Deli sandwiches are the main lunch fare at Schilo's, and you've got lots of choices. From reubens to vegetarian style, tuna salad to good ol' peanut butter and jelly, the menu lists more than 30 sandwiches, including Schilo's Burger (a large patty on a poppy seed bun). Daily lunch specials feature beef stew, corned beef, meat loaf, chicken and dumplings, roast beef and gravy, and hamburger steak.

For an authentic German supper, dine at Schilo's in the evening. Then you can choose from wiener schnitzel (breaded and fried pork loin), bratwurst (veal and pork sausage), jaeger schnitzel (pork loin with mushroom gravy), fricadelle (German chopped sirloin with mushroom gravy), sauerbraten (roast sirloin with sweet and sour gravy), and Vienna paprika chicken (diced chicken breast and noodles with paprika gravy).

Wash it all down with a frosty mug of Schilo's famous root beer. Or, better yet, share a fudge nut brownie with a scoop of Blue Bell ice cream.

Ice cream at a deli? Well, sure. That's a delicacy, too!

Gettin' there: From I-37/U.S. 281, exit Commerce Street. Turn west on Commerce. Schilo's is at 424 E. Commerce St. Parking is available in a next-door garage or turn left on Presa Street, then left on Market Street. You can park in the Casa Rio parking lot. Expect to pay for parking anywhere you go in downtown San Antonio.

Schilo's
424 E. Commerce St.
San Antonio, TX
210/223-6692

Stop by and see: See the Alamo. Need I say more???

Schilo's Miss Irma's Apple Streusel
Step 1:
½ cup butter
2 cups sugar
3 eggs

Cream butter and sugar until well blended. Add eggs, one at a time; mix until blended.

Step 2:
4 cups flour
2 teaspoons apple pie spice
2 teaspoons baking soda

Sift flour, apple pie spice, and baking soda together.

Step 3:
1 ½ pints buttermilk

Add dry mixture to creamed mixture, alternately adding buttermilk. Mix until blended.

Step 4:
60 ounces sliced apples for pies (it's very important that you get apples for pies—they're crisper and will hold up during cooking.)

Pour buttermilk mixture into a 10x15-inch greased and floured pan. Top with apples slices. Place in a 325-degree oven while preparing streusel topping.

Step 5:
1 cup flour
1 cup sugar
1 tablespoon apple pie spice
½ cup butter, melted

Combine sugar, flour, and apple pie spice. Gradually add melted butter until blended. Place on top of apples and continue baking for 1½ hours at 325 degrees until done. After removing from oven, sprinkle top of streusel with a light coat of granulated sugar.

Schulenburg

Frank's Restaurant
(1929)

If you've ever traveled the highway between San Antonio and Houston, then you know Frank's. The roadside establishment has been feeding travelers for more than seven decades.

Frank and Rozine Tilicek originally opened the restaurant in 1929. Back then, a burger cost a dime. Today, Frank's Original Jumbo Schulenburger goes for nearly three bucks. They may cost more, but the burgers at Frank's sell just as fast now as they did then.

Besides burgers and sandwiches, Frank's also serves steaks, fried chicken, shrimp and catfish, breaded beef cutlets, chili, chicken-fried steak, and enchiladas. Homemade pies, like Dutch apple and lemon meringue, are the restaurant's specialty.

A gift shop at one end of the restaurant sells lots of Texas souvenirs, cookbooks, and an assortment of packaged eats.

Gettin' there: Frank's Restaurant is located on the south side of I-10 at Schulenburg.

Frank's Restaurant
P.O. Box 1
Schulenburg, TX 78956
409/743-3555

Stop by and see: Take a "painted churches" tour. Churches in Dubina, Ammannsville, Praha, and High Hill feature hand-painted murals, frescoes, and other historic art. For more information, call 409/743-4514.

Victoria

Fossati's Delicatessen
(1882)

In this collection of roadside restaurants, Fossati's ranks as the oldest. The Victoria deli, which opened in 1882, is likely the oldest delicatessen in the state.

Its history begins with Frank Napoleon Fossati, an Italian stone cutter born in 1852. He arrived at Ellis Island in 1880 and headed west after hearing artisans were needed to build the Texas state capitol. Alas, the massive project was still in its planning stages so Fossati headed west again and worked as a laborer on a bridge construction crew on the Pecos River. Later, he moved to Victoria and worked in a marble yard until he quit on doctor's orders. Not one to sit still long, Fossati in March 1882 opened a chili-and-sandwich stand at the corner of Main and Juan Linn Streets. In 1895 he and a partner opened a combination bar, restaurant, and imported food business at 220 S. Main St. Seven years later Fossati, a successful and well-respected businessman by this time, opened Fossati's Grocery and Feed Store at 302 S. Main, its present-day location. In 1910 Fossati bequeathed the business to his oldest son, Caeton, who kept it going until he retired in 1967. Others ran the deli until it closed in 1981. It wasn't long before Fossati's descendants purchased the unpretentious clapboard building and reopened part of Victoria's heritage and theirs.

Old-time photographs recalling bygone days hang on walls throughout Fossati's. Customers enjoy the historic atmosphere as well as the food at the deli, which serves oodles of sandwiches (turkey poorboys, pita clubs, tuna melts, kraut dogs, and reubens, to name a few), two kinds of soups, and several salads. A tribute to the family's Italian roots, Fossati's Italian Spaghetti with meat sauce comes with a salad and garlic bread.

For folks on the go, Fossati's also offers brown bag specials—literally. Brown Bag II comes with a half sandwich, potato pasta or coleslaw salad, and a brownie. Brown Bag III comes with choice of chicken or tuna salad sandwich, chips, a pickle, and one of Fossati's chocolate chip cookies.

Pop into Fossati's for a root beer and sandwich, and you'll be glad you did.

Gettin' there: From Loop 463, exit onto the Cuero highway (U.S. 87). This runs into downtown and turns into Main Street. Fossati's is located at the corner of Main and Juan Linn Streets.

Fossati's Delicatessen
302 S. Main St.
Victoria, TX 77901
361/576-3354

Stop by and see: The Texas Zoo in Riverside Park exhibits native Texas species in natural environments.

German Potato Salad

5 pounds red potatoes
5 strips bacon
1 onion, chopped
2 tablespoons flour
2 tablespoons sugar
1 ½ teaspoons salt
1 teaspoon pepper
½ cup vinegar
½ cup water

Wash and scrub red potatoes. Leaving skin on, boil, cool and dice. Saute diced bacon with onion until onion is tender. To the bacon and onion mixture, add flour, sugar, salt, and pepper; stir well. Then add vinegar and water. Toss sauce with potatoes. Serve warm. Serves 15-20.

Broccoli Cheese Soup

2 packages frozen chopped broccoli
2 quarts chicken broth
1 cup margarine
1 ¼ cups flour
1 teaspoon salt

½ teaspoon white pepper
1 teaspoon cumin
3 pints half-and-half
processed cheese sauce

Combine frozen broccoli with chicken broth and bring to a
boil. Melt margarine and stir in flour; mix with wire whisk.
Add salt, pepper, and cumin; stir well. Add half-and-half to
flour mixture and stir with wire whisk. Add cream sauce to
broccoli and chicken broth when broccoli is done. To this
add processed cheese sauce to desired taste. Yields approximately 20 servings.

Weesatche

Weesatche Cafe
(1900)

"You wouldn't have an inklin' this place was here unless someone took ya," proclaimed Dick Phelps as we pulled off Texas
119 and stopped in front of the Weesatche Cafe.

Yep. He was right. I'd never even heard of the town (named
for the huisache tree and pronounced the same way) until Dick
and his wife, Margaret, drove out of their way from Victoria to
buy me lunch there. From the run-down looks of the cafe, constructed of weathered barn wood, not too many other folks had
heard of the place either. Or so I thought.

"Doesn't it look like Dodge City?" asked Margaret, as we
stepped onto the porch and headed inside. Minus a glass-
sliding door, the building could easily pose as an Old West
storefront in Matt Dillon's legendary town.

"Make ya'self at home!" announced a large woman holding
a stack of plastic-covered menus. She laid one in front of us as
we plunked down in vinyl-covered chairs and scooted up to the
worn, Formica-topped table shoved up against the wall. My
chair had orange vinyl. Dick's had lemon yellow.

Not much of anything matches or coordinates here. Seafoam green and mint-candy yellow covers what wall space peeks out from behind calendars, assorted pictures, a few neon signs, and a high shelf laden with stuff. The same yellow paint covers the bar where folks can stand and sip ice-cold sodas, which sell fast in the summer when only ceiling fans and a huge box fan beat back the heat.

No matter the temperature, locals and out-of-towners regularly frequent this roadhouse, built around 1900 and added onto three times. "We've got 'em coming from Corpus and San Antonio, London and California," claimed Nadine Borgfeld, the cafe's owner and number one cook. "We're famous for our battered fries and homemade chili. We don't open a can. Everything's from scratch."

Speaking of food, Nadine, who waitressed as a teenager here and later bought the business from her former mother-in-law, serves a modest breakfast selection of eggs, taquitos, and doughnuts. For lunch, a big pile of her famous fries almost dwarfs their plate mate, a thick burger wrapped in tissue paper. I couldn't finish the fries but wished I could. Lightly battered and crisply fried, the thin strips of potatoes didn't glisten at all with even a hint of grease. The daily lunch special (priced so low you won't believe it) includes a meat like hamburger steak or glazed ham, two veggie sides, tea, and a small slice of the day's featured pie (lemon meringue, coconut, banana, or chocolate). Fried chicken, steak dinners, and Mexican food entice evening diners.

Across the street stands the abandoned one-room Weesatche jail, constructed of the same weathered barn wood. Folks won't mind if you open the door and stick your head in a minute to see the bare walls and the built-in, one-holer. The sight might even stir up a bit of sympathy for those who had to stay a night or more.

Then again, maybe not.

Gettin' there: From Goliad, head north on U.S. 183, then west on Texas 119 about 5 miles to Weesatche. Turn west on Main Street.

Weesatche Cafe
Highway 884
Weesatche, TX 77993

Homemade Coleslaw Dressing

1 cup salad dressing
½ teaspoon garlic salt
½ teaspoon celery salt
½ teaspoon onion salt
¼ cup vinegar
½ cup sugar

Mix all above. Also makes a good salad dressing.

Nadine's Barbecued Chicken

4 whole chickens
yellow mustard
salt
pepper
garlic powder

Cut chickens in half. Sprinkle salt, pepper, and garlic powder on cut-up chicken. Spread mustard on both sides of chicken. Throw this on your barbecue grill or pit. Turn every 30 minutes until chicken is done. About 1 hour.

Nadine's Homemade Barbecue Sauce

2 8-ounce cans tomato sauce
Worcestershire sauce to taste
½ cup brown sugar
½ medium onion, diced

Bring all ingredients to a rolling boil. Also good on barbecue ribs or pork chops.

Update: Unfortunately, at the time of publication, this hole-in-the-wall heaven had closed its doors. But the recipes are great and worth including in the book.

Other old-time restaurants:

Corpus Christi
Angelo's Pizza & Hamburgers (1956)
3619 S. Staples St.
Corpus Christi, TX 78411
361/853-2181

Old Mexico Restaurant (1954)
3329 Leopard St.
Corpus Christi, TX 78408
361/883-6461

Astor Restaurant (1957)
5533 Leopard St.
Corpus Christi, TX 78408
361/289-0101

U & I Family Restaurant (1972)
309 S. Water St.
Corpus Christi, TX 78401
361/883-3492

Donna
Harold's Country Kitchen (1960)
2111 U.S. Highway 83
Donna, TX 78537
956/464-2185

Falls City
Palace Cafe (1923)
300 Front St.
Box 6
Falls City, TX 78113
830/254-3414

Laredo
Glass Kitchen (1952)
302 Corpus Christi St.
Laredo, TX 78040
956/722-2822

Marion
Goerke's Country Tavern (1971)
1901 Weil Rd.
Marion, TX 78124
830/914-2521

Rockport
Big Fisherman Restaurant (1972)
510 Highway 188
Rockport, TX 78382
361/729-1997

Charlotte Plummer's Seafare
Restaurant (mid 1970s)
202 N. Fulton Beach Rd.
Rockport, TX 78382
361/729-1185

Kline's Cafe (1963)
106 S. Austin St.
Rockport, TX 78382
361/729-8538

San Antonio

Barn Door Restaurant (1953)
8400 N. New Braunfels Ave.
San Antonio, TX 78209
210/824-0116

Hung Fong Chinese Restaurant (1939)
3624 Broadway
San Antonio, TX 78209
210/822-9211

Jacala Mexican Restaurant (1949)
606 West Ave.
San Antonio, TX 78201
210/732-5222

La Fonda (1932)
2415 N. Main Ave.
San Antonio, TX 78212
210/733-0621

Malt House (1947)
115 S. Zarzamora St.
San Antonio, TX 78207
210/433-8441

San Juan

Garza Cafe (1943)
308 N. Nebraska
San Juan, TX 78589
956/787-9051

Seguin

El Ranchito (early 1940s)
983 N. Highway 123 Byp.
Seguin, TX 78155
830/303-7802

South Padre Island

Ro-Van's Bakery & Restaurant (1969)
5300 Padre Blvd.
South Padre Island, TX 78597
956/761-6972

Weslaco

Keno's Cafe (1933)
253 S. Texas Blvd.
Weslaco, TX 78596
956/968-2474

Over in the east

Beaumont

Don's Seafood & Steak House
(1968)

This saga of a family-owned group of seafood restaurants crosses state lines. Don's Seafood & Steak House traces its start back to 1934 when Don L. Landry, whose ancestors were Acadians from Nova Scotia, opened a tiny French-Acadian restaurant known as Don's Beer Parlor in Lafayette, Louisiana. Don's brother Ashby joined the business five years later. Excellent food and friendly service earned the restaurant more customers, and the restaurant grew. With the addition of more seafood to the menu, the brothers changed the restaurant's name to Don's Seafood Inn. In 1952 brother Willie merged his corner grocery store with his siblings' restaurant, and the name changed—for a final time—to Don's Seafood & Steak House. As more and more Landry family members joined the business, other Don's restaurants opened in Louisiana and Texas. The Beaumont location opened in 1968. In Louisiana, Don's Seafood & Steak Houses are located in Baton Rouge, Hammond, Lafayette, and Shreveport.

Best known for their spicy Cajun cuisine, the chefs at Don's prepare only the freshest shrimp, crab, oysters, flounder, crawfish, trout, and red snapper. The extensive menu includes fried oysters, stuffed crab, crabmeat au gratin, crawfish etouffee, shrimp creole, gumbos galore, and more more more. There's also a selection of steaks and chicken platters.

But who wants to eat steak when there's fried shrimp on the menu?

Gettin' there: Don's is located at I-10 and Washington Boulevard.

Don's Seafood & Steak House
2290 Interstate 10 S.
Beaumont, TX 77707
409/842-0686

Stop by and see: Texas got its start in the oil industry in the
Beaumont area back in 1901. That's when the famous Lucas
Gusher blew in atop a mound known as Spindletop Hill. Today,
a pink granite monument commemorating the gusher stands at
the Spindletop/Gladys City Boomtown Museum (Highways
69, 96, and 287 at University Drive), a complex of replica clapboard buildings constructed as a bicentennial project in the
mid-1970s. A blacksmith shop, barber shop, livery stable, general store, drug store, and 10 other buildings represent life in
Gladys City around the turn of the century.

The following recipes are from the cookbook *Secrets of the
Original Don's Seafood & Steakhouse,* first published as *Don's
Secrets* in 1958.

Hush Puppies
1 pint flour
1 pint cornmeal
3 tablespoons sugar
1 tablespoon salt
2 tablespoons baking powder
½ cup green onions, chopped fine
½ pint onions, chopped fine
1 teaspoon or to taste cayenne (red pepper)
4 eggs
12 ounces milk

Mix all ingredients together well, adding milk last. Using a
scoop, drop portions of the mixture into hot oil and fry until
the hush puppy floats. Makes 64 hush puppies.

Tartar Sauce
1 quart mayonnaise
½ pint sweet relish
1 teaspoon dry mustard
3 tablespoons cold water
1 teaspoon white vinegar
½ cup ground onions (very fine)

Mix all ingredients together in a bowl. Serve with fried sea-food or salad. Makes 1 ½ quarts.

Trout Almondine

4 pounds fresh trout, cleaned
1 egg
½ pint milk
¼ pound butter
1 5-ounce can almonds
½ cup cold water
¼ cup parsley, chopped
½ teaspoon cornstarch
1 cup all-purpose flour
salt, black pepper, and cayenne
cooking oil

Beat egg and milk together. Set aside. Split trout lengthwise. Season generously with salt, black pepper, and cayenne. Dip in egg and milk mixture, then roll in flour. Put ½ inch of cooking oil in a heavy pot over high heat. Fry trout, uncovered. When trout is golden brown on both sides, remove and set aside.

Grind almonds and put in a heavy skillet with butter. Fry over medium heat, uncovered, until almonds are brown. Drain off ⅔ of the butter. Dissolve cornstarch in ½ cup cold water and add to the fried almonds. Season with salt, black pepper, and cayenne to taste. Pour this mixture over fried trout. Garnish with parsley. Serves 4.

Stuffed Shrimp

1 pound fresh shrimp, peeled and deveined
1 pound backfin crabmeat
2 eggs
1 cup onions, chopped
½ cup celery, chopped
¼ pound oleo or ½ cup cooking oil
½ cup green onions and parsley, chopped fine
½ cup tomato catsup
½ cup bread crumbs
¼ cup bell pepper, chopped
2 stale hamburger buns or 3 slices stale bread
salt, black pepper
cayenne to taste
½ pound boiled shrimp, peeled and deveined

119

Set fresh shrimp aside after peeling. Put oil or oleo, onions, and ¼ cup of the chopped celery into a heavy pot. Season to taste with salt, black pepper, and cayenne. Cook slowly, uncovered, until onions are wilted. To wilted vegetables, add tomato catsup. Mix well. Grind boiled shrimp in food chopper. Mix shrimp and crabmeat with onion mixture and cook 15 minutes over medium heat in an uncovered pot. Add buns, which have been soaked in eggs; mix well. Add bell pepper, remainder of celery, green onions, parsley, and bread crumbs. Mix well.

Split each fresh shrimp lengthwise, almost to the end and flatten out. Stuff centers of split shrimp with mixture, holding each shrimp in the hand and squeezing together to form a croquette. Roll in all-purpose flour. Then dip in heavy egg batter (recipe follows) and roll in bread crumbs. Fry rapidly for 5 minutes in deep fat at 375 degrees. Serves 5.

Heavy Egg Batter

2 beaten eggs
pinch of salt
½ cup evaporated milk

Mix all ingredients well.

Pig Stand
(1923)

What do Texas toast, fluorescent lighting, and drive-through windows have in common? The famous family of Pig Stand restaurants, that's what.

The original Pig Stand opened in 1921 in Dallas, and the first one in Beaumont in 1923 (it was later torn down). But Beaumont likes to tout its Calder Street location, built in 1943, as the most famous. After all, thick-sliced Texas Toast got its start there. Pig Stands were also the first restaurants to use fluorescent and neon lighting, drive-through windows, and air conditioning. And by the way, ever heard of fried onion rings? A cook at a Pig Stand invented those, too.

Back in the twenties, Americans had never considered eating IN their Model Ts. That would change forever when Dr. R.W. Jackson and businessman J.G. Kirby opened the first Pig Stand in Dallas. Their novel idea—convenient, curbside meals—instantly appealed to motorists. They wouldn't even have to get out of their cars! Instead, teenaged waiters would hop on running boards, take orders for Pig Sandwiches and ice-cold sodas, then return just as quickly with the food (now you know where the term "carhop" originated). Customers loved the new restaurant, which spurred the partners to start 60 more throughout the southern United States. Other fast-food eateries cropped up along the way, and, well, you know the rest of that story.

Today, seven Pig Stands survive—one in Houston, three in Beaumont, and three in San Antonio. A brand new Pig Stand opened in Lytle in 1999. In Beaumont, No. 41 on Calder Street, built in 1943, stands as perhaps the nation's oldest circular drive-in. Inside, regular customers as well as the sentimental at heart fill up the booths and stools at the counter. They come 'cause they're addicted to the crispy chicken-fried steak sandwiches (another first in the industry for Pig Stands), king-sized hamburgers, and those trademarked Pig Sandwiches (succulent slices of barbecued pork served on a bun and tucked into tissue). They come to reminiscence about the good ol' days when they hung out there as teenagers, slurped on malts, and checked out the dating scene.

They come to feel good, inside and out.

Gettin' there: From I-10 West, take the Calder Exit and turn east onto Calder. Go about 2 miles. Cross the railroad tracks and the Pig Stand's on your right. From the east on I-10, take the Martin Luther King Parkway exit. At the traffic light, turn left and go under I-10. Stay on MLK Parkway until you get to Calder Street. Turn right. Restaurant's on your left.

Pig Stand
1595 Calder
Beaumont, TX 77701
409/813-1444

Stop by and see: The McFaddin-Ward House at 1906 Calder Ave. showcases the wealthy lifestyle of a South Texas family during the early 1900s.

Pig Stand's Texas-size Donuts and Glaze

1½ pounds International Donut Base
1½ pounds flour
3 cups water
3 ounces yeast

Dissolve yeast in lukewarm water Add flour and International Donut Base. Mix at slow speed for 2 minutes, then fast speed for 5 minutes. Knead lightly. Place in floured pan for proofing. Use 3½-inch donut cutter. Deep fry at 365 degrees until golden brown. Makes 33 donuts (each approximately 7 inches in diameter).

Glaze:
2 cups Simply Syrup
1 tablespoon Sta-Frost
2 pounds powdered sugar
1 teaspoon imitation vanilla

Warm simple syrup slightly. Dissolve Sta-Frost in warm syrup. Blend in sugar and whip until smooth. Add vanilla. Donuts must be glazed while still hot. Glaze on both sides.

Coleslaw and Dressing
2 heads cabbage, grated
1 slice (⅜ to ½ inch thick) purple cabbage, finely chopped
one pod pimento, finely chopped

Dressing:
1 quart salad dressing
¾ cup sugar
½ cup Heinz vinegar
1 teaspoon white pepper
1 teaspoon salt

Blend and mix all ingredients.

Quality Cafe
(1930)

An Italian immigrant by the name of Batiste Girolamo originally opened the Quality Cafe in 1930. He ran the restaurant for 50 years, then sold the downtown business to Helen and Sam Danna, who've kept the cafe going ever since.

One of the traditions they've kept alive is the Quality Plate Lunch Special, served Monday through Friday. The special includes your choice of one meat, two vegetables, a salad, and dessert. Thursdays, for instance, feature meatballs, fried chicken, and beef tips. Vegetables include steamed rice, northern beans, buttered corn, spinach, and creamed potatoes. Salad offerings are potato salad, beets, or a tossed salad. And for dessert, there's bread pudding.

The menu also serves up a selection of burgers, sandwiches, plate meals (fried chicken, catfish, pork chops, and chicken-fried steak), and several "heart healthy" choices, like marinated catfish, chicken breast and shrimp, tuna salad, shrimp pasta salad, vegetable soup, and a bowl of fresh fruit.

For breakfast, the restaurant serves omelettes, pancakes, waffles, and cinnamon rolls. All breakfast specials include buttermilk biscuits, "a mainstay of the Quality Cafe since 1965," claims the menu.

Speaking of menus, the Quality Cafe has had some unusual covers over the years. One illustrated menu cover features a hand-sketched plane about to land near the cafe's front door. Another cartoon-like drawing shows two cars parked out front and people on their way inside the cafe. A third promotes the local football team ("Go Falcons"), and yet another is decorated with photographs of grinning high school students.

"Our customers did the artwork," Helen Danna explains. "Most people get a big kick out of looking at them."

Gettin' there: From I-10, take the Downtown exit. You will be on Willow Street. Go four blocks to Liberty Street. Federal courthouse will be on the right. Take a left; it is the first building on the left.

Quality Cafe
730 Liberty St.
Beaumont, TX 77701
409/835-9652

The cafe's Thursday special . . .

Meatballs and Spaghetti
Meatballs:
5 pounds cubed beef meat, lean

1 pound cubed pork meat, lean
(or use ground meat—80 percent lean beef and
20 percent lean pork)
1 head garlic
½ bunch parsley
½ loaf white bread or French bread, soaked
in 1 cup milk
4 eggs
2 tablespoons salt
1 tablespoon pepper

Use meat grinder. Grind meat with first five ingredients. As you add bread, squeeze the milk out. Mix meat mixture thoroughly. Add eggs, salt, and pepper. Portion mixture into 4-ounce pieces. Oil hands. Roll meat into firm balls. Place in baking pan, add a small amount of water, and bake at 325 degrees for approximately 1 hour.

Sauce:
2 20-ounce cans tomato paste (plus 4 cans water)
2 20-ounce cans crushed tomatoes (plus 4 cans water)
4 ribs celery, chopped
1 small bell pepper, chopped
1 jumbo onion, chopped
1 head of garlic, divided into cloves, then minced
½ cup sugar (or to taste)
¼ bunch parsley, chopped
4 sprigs basil, chopped

In a large pot, saute onion, pepper, celery, and garlic in a small amount of olive oil. Add tomato paste and crushed tomatoes. Add the water, season with salt, pepper, and sugar. Add parsley and basil. Cook on low for 2 to 3 hours, stirring frequently. Add meatballs in the last hour. Serve over spaghetti. Feeds a crowd.

Gumbo
2 or 3 pounds shrimp (70-90 count)

Boil shrimp in seasoned water (to taste with salt, pepper, TexJoy Steak Seasoning, garlic powder, and Tabasco sauce) for approximately 4 minutes. Remove shrimp and set shrimp water aside.

Roux:
1 cup flour
1 cup oil

Cook in pan until brown, stirring often. Be sure not to scorch.

Add to roux:
1 large onion, chopped
3 ribs celery, chopped
4 cloves garlic, chopped
1 small bell pepper, chopped
1 tablespoon filé

Stir until the vegetables are well coated with roux. Add roux mixture to shrimp water and stir thoroughly. Cook at least 1 hour on low. Add shrimp; cook about 5 minutes. Serve over hot rice.

The cafe's Friday special . . .

Shrimp and Okra Gumbo

We also add okra and tomato to our gumbo for a different taste.

Saute one small onion in a small amount of oil. Add 1 pound okra (chopped) and 1 20-ounce can tomatoes. Cook about 10 minutes. Add to the gumbo and boil about 1 hour.

Shrimp Pasta Salad

1½ pounds vermicelli
1½ pounds small shrimp (70-90 count)
3 green onions, chopped
1 20-ounce can sliced black olives
6 eggs, hard boiled and chopped
fresh dillweed

Boil pasta 4 minutes. Add 1 teaspoon salt and 1 tablespoon oil to water. Drain; do not rinse. Add ¼ cup oil, ¼ cup lemon juice, and 1 teaspoon dill to the pasta. Toss pasta and set aside to marinate.

Boil shrimp in seasoned water (salt, pepper, Tabasco sauce, TexJoy Steak or Seafood Seasoning, and garlic powder) until just done. Do not overcook. Drain. Toss together the pasta, shrimp, onions, olives, and eggs.

Mix sauce: ½ cup oil, ½ cup mayonnaise, ⅓ cup lemon juice, 3 tablespoons TexJoy Steak Seasoning, and 1 cup Leo's Italian Dressing. Add sauce to pasta mixture and toss. Keep refrigerated.

Thursday's featured dessert...

Bread Pudding

1 quart whole milk
6 eggs
1 cup sugar
1 teaspoon vanilla
½ teaspoon salt
1 loaf French bread

Mix first five ingredients together. Tear bread into small pieces and add to mixture. Pour into baking pan that has been sprayed with Pam. Sprinkle butter, sugar, and cinnamon over top. Place in a pan of water and bake approximately 1 hour at 350 degrees. Cool and serve with vanilla cream sauce.

Vanilla cream sauce:
2 cups milk
1 cup sugar
2 tablespoons cornstarch
½ teaspoon salt
3 egg yolks
1 teaspoon vanilla
1 tablespoon butter

Mix first four ingredients together. Cook, stirring constantly, until it starts to boil. Add egg yolks that have been beaten with a small amount of hot sauce. Mix together and add to hot sauce and cook 30 seconds, stirring constantly. Remove from heat and add butter and vanilla. Cool and serve over bread pudding.

Burton

Burton Cafe
(1937)

At the Burton Cafe, the early 1980s stand out as pretty good years. Folks who've lived there awhile remember 1983 as the year J.R. came to town. In fact, some people still have the fake hundred-dollar bills actor Larry Hagman passed out when he and his friends flew in by helicopter to check on his oil investments in the area. The group ate lunch at the Burton Cafe, and Larry, best known for his role as the suave and scandalous J.R. Ewing on *Dallas*, autographed the chair he sat in. He also gave away the souvenir bills with his photograph on them, and one still hangs in the cafe. The next year, a new city sewage treatment plant kicking into operation was a happy event for the Burton Cafe. Completion of the project meant the cafe owners could build modern restrooms, a welcome replacement for the age-old outhouses nearly hidden in the rose bushes. Hence, a sign above the restroom doors inside the Burton Cafe reads "In Houses."

The year 1984 is also fondly recalled because that's the year *Texas Monthly* magazine declared the Burton Cafe as one of the eight best "country cafes" in the state.

The Burton Cafe originally opened in 1937 after a previous cafe burned down across the street. Subsequent restaurant managers followed through the years. In 1966 a wall separating the "all-white" dining area from the black was removed. In 1991 Steve and Cindy Miller from Houston bought the cafe. They've continued the tradition of good food, and people come from miles to eat the Millers' T-bone steaks, chicken-fried steaks, fried catfish, burgers, and beer-battered onion rings. Save room for the cafe's specialty—a slice of coconut cream pie. There's also chocolate, lemon meringue, buttermilk, apple, peach, and strawberry pies, served with—what else this close to Brenham??—a scoop of Blue Bell Homemade Vanilla ice cream.

Everything's cooked to order here. "So please remember, folks," the menu advises, "home cooking is worth the wait!"

Bonus: The Burton Cafe has its own Texas Historical Marker. Check it out.

Gettin' there: Burton is 12 miles west of Brenham, about one mile north of U.S. 290 on FM 390. The Burton Cafe is one block west of Main Street on Washington Street.

Burton Cafe
12513 Washington St.
Burton, TX 77835
409/289-3849

Stop by and see: The Burton Farmers Gin is a National Historic Landmark. It was built in 1914 and powered by a 1925 Bessemer twin type IV oil engine. Also, if you have the time, GET TO BRENHAM QUICK! Why? Blue Bell Creameries, naturally! Take a tour and enjoy a cone of the delicious stuff. There's even a gift shop. Located off U.S. 290 on FM 577 (southeast of downtown Brenham).

Burton Cafe's Pecan Pie

1 cup sugar
1 cup light corn syrup
$\frac{1}{3}$ cup melted butter or oleo
dash salt
$\frac{1}{2}$ teaspoon vanilla
4 eggs
1 $\frac{1}{4}$ cups chopped pecans
9-inch pie shell, unbaked

Cream together first five ingredients, then whisk in the eggs until well blended. Put the chopped pecans in the unbaked pie shell and pour the sugar mixture over the pecans. Bake at 350 degrees for approximately one hour.

Burton Cafe's Buttermilk Pie

1 $\frac{1}{2}$ cups sugar

1 tablespoon flour
1 tablespoon cornstarch
dash salt
4 eggs
$\frac{1}{4}$ cup melted butter
1 cup buttermilk
$\frac{1}{2}$ teaspoon vanilla
$\frac{1}{4}$ cup coconut
9-inch pie shell, unbaked

Combine first four ingredients. Whisk in eggs, butter, buttermilk, and vanilla. Sprinkle coconut in bottom of unbaked pie shell and pour liquid mixture over top. Bake at 350 degrees for 1 hour until lightly browned and puffed up.

Texas Historical Marker Burton Cafe

Built in 1937 by Edward Whitener and Quintus Zwernemann, this cafe has been a popular feature of downtown Burton through the years. Serving as both a cafe and social center for generations, it also included a liquor store at one time. Outdoor bathroom facilities were replaced in 1984. Its simple architectural features include a false front stepped parapet sheathed in metal stamped in a brick pattern.

Centerville

Town Cafe

(1939)

The Town Cafe on Highway 75 has been in business continuously since 1939. "It's never been closed that I know of," says owner Kathy Johnson.

Hand-breaded chicken-fried steaks and crisp fried chicken are among the restaurant's specialties. "We also grind our meat for our burgers and hand cut our rib eyes," Kathy adds. "We make our own homemade sausage, too. People love it."

The sausage is served in the morning at breakfast, as a side order or with eggs and pancakes. At noon and in the evening, the cafe's menu features salads, chili, a soup of the day, burgers, sandwiches, and plate meals, such as chopped sirloin with grilled onions and mushrooms, pork chops, roast beef, and catfish. A popular lunch buffet is served Monday through Thursday.

Gettin' there: Centerville is located 80 miles west of Lufkin off Interstate 45.

Town Cafe
Hwy. 75 South
P.O. Box 468
Centerville 75833
903/536-2919

Stop by and see: The Leon County courthouse, built in 1887, is one of the oldest such buildings in Texas.

Galveston

Gaido's Seafood Restaurant
(1911)

Ellis Island and the Statute of Liberty symbolize the massive immigration movement of the 1800s and early 1900s. But did you know that Galveston Island ranked second behind Ellis Island as an immigration station? Yep, it's true.

Among the immigrants who arrived in Galveston before the turn of the century was an Italian by the name of San Jacinto Gaido. In 1911 he opened a hamburger and hot dog stand atop Murdoch's Bathhouse, which stood on the beach overlooking the water. In 1937 the Gaido family moved the restaurant to its present location on Seawall Boulevard. One of his three sons, Mike, later took over the restaurant and turned it into a landmark. So much, in fact, that in 1998 *Texas Highways* readers voted the Galveston eatery as THE best restaurant in the state while *Southern Living* readers credited Gaido's as serving the "best seafood on the Gulf Coast."

In Galveston, you can't miss Gaido's. On Seawall Boulevard, it's the brick building with the big blue crab perched on the roof, a real attention-getter that attests to the restaurant's commitment to serving only the freshest seafood caught in the Gulf. Next door, a huge pink shrimp, perched on a pole, guards Gaido's sibling restaurant, the laid-back (and less expensive) Casey's, a 50-plus-year-old business. The family's two-block complex overlooking the bay also encompasses Gaido's Seaside Inn, a 102-room motel built in the 1950s.

Both customers and employees are almost fixtures at Gaido's. Raymond Campbell, known as Captain Ray, has worked as a waiter there for more than 50 years. He started at the age of 17 after Mike Gaido hired him away from the Hotel Galvez. Many other employees have worked at Gaido's for more than 30 and 40 years. Customers, too, are staunchly loyal. One couple, for instance, has eaten at Gaido's annually for more than 55 years. They honeymooned in Galveston in the early 1940s, shared a romantic dinner at the restaurant, and have returned every year ever since.

If true love—like that of the devoted couple—had flavor, it'd taste like the exquisitely prepared shrimp, oysters, scallops, and red snapper served at Gaido's. Besides fried, charcoal grilled, and blackened selections, chefs also prepare seafood using their signature methods, called "Michael" (dusted in crushed crackers and seasoned flour, pan sauteed in butter), "Sapporito" (dusted in crushed crackers and garlic, then sauteed), and "Wade" (dusted in seasoned flour, then sauteed). Some entrees, like baked or fried flounder, take as long as a half hour to cook, and the menu advises accordingly.

What's truly amazing, though, is the number of people Gaido's serves every year—more than 350,000. San Jacinto Gaido would be amazed.

Gettin' there: From I-45, stay on Broadway, then turn right on 39th Street, which ends at Seawall Boulevard.

Gaido's
3800 Seawall Blvd.
Galveston, TX 77556
409/762-9625

Stop by and see: The pyramids you see coming across the causeway are part of Moody Gardens, a 156-acre complex. The Rainforest Pyramid, the largest of the trio, showcases the flora and fauna of Asian, African, and South American rainforests. The pink-colored Discovery Pyramid houses exhibits developed in conjunction with NASA's Johnson Space Center plus an IMAX Ridefilm Theater. The blue Aquarium Pyramid contains 1.5 million gallons of water in four major marine habitat exhibits.

Gaido's Oysters Ponzini

8 fluid ounces chicken stock
1 pound yellow onions, chopped fine
1 1/4 pounds mushrooms, chopped fine
1 2/3 cups heavy cream
3 fluid ounces dry white wine
1 pound sliced Swiss cheese
2 1/2 cups Parmesan cheese
1 teaspoon cayenne pepper
1/2 teaspoon salt
1/4 teaspoon nutmeg
4-5 egg yolks, depending on size of eggs

Preparation:

Caramelize onions by slowly sauteing in frying pan until very brown. In kettle, place chicken base, caramelized onions, nutmeg, salt, mushrooms, wine, cayenne pepper, and heavy cream. Bring almost to a boil. Turn off heat. Add Swiss cheese, slice by slice, and mix thoroughly until Swiss cheese has melted and been completely incorporated into the mixture. Add Parmesan cheese. Mix thoroughly until Parmesan cheese has been completely incorporated.

Add egg yolks. Mix in well. Continue to cook on low heat until the mixture is thick.

It is best to make the Ponzini sauce a day or two before you plan to serve this. Once the oysters have been shucked (try to have the oyster remain in the larger of the two shells), clean the shells inside and out without actually removing the oyster from the shell. Spoon the mixture on top of the oysters.

This makes enough sauce for 45-60 oysters (1 ounce of sauce for each oyster). Preheat oven to 350 degrees. Place oysters in oven and cook until sauce is bubbly and oysters cooked. Because oysters vary in size, it is best to cut into one of the oysters to ensure doneness. Cooking time is approximately 15 minutes.

Pecan Crunch Pie

5 eggs
1 ½ cups sugar
1 ¾ cups plus ¼ cup Karo Light Corn Syrup
2 teaspoons vanilla extract
¼ teaspoon salt
2 ½ cups pecan pieces, toasted
2 ½ cups pecan halves, toasted

Graham cracker crust:
1 ½ cups graham crackers, ground finely
7 tablespoons sugar
2 tablespoons butter, melted

To assemble crust: butter the inside of a 10-inch spring-form pan. Combine crust ingredients. Cover the base of the spring-form pan with the mixture. Make pie by mixing eggs in a bowl. Then add sugar, 1 ¾ cups syrup, vanilla, and salt. Mix well. Stir in 2 ½ cups of toasted pecan pieces. Pour into prepared crust. Bake in oven that has been preheated to 300 degrees for approximately one hour.

Pecan pies are "done" when pie is soft to the touch in the center and firm around the outside edges. Allow pie to cool on a rack. When cooled slightly, about one hour, remove sides from pan. Then turn pie upside down and remove bottom of pan.

Place mixture of toasted pecan halves and ¼-cup syrup on top surface of upside down pie to form an even, single layer of pecans.

Sonny's Place
(1944)

"Behave or be gone."

For more than fifty years, those stern words of warning have hung on the wall and graced the menu cover at Sonny's Place on 19th Street. Lawrence Puccetti Sr. in 1930 bought the old 1886 building, which at the time housed a number of seedy "speakeasies" and gambling casinos. In 1944 he evicted the last one and opened Sonny's Place, named for one of his sons who served in the Navy during World War II.

According to one old menu, Lawrence Sr. took great pride in offering a family atmosphere to his customers, not to mention great food and the coldest beer in Galveston. Theresa, his wife, cooked most of the food, which included her family recipes of spaghetti and meatballs, veal cutlets, lasagna, and smothered chicken. Friday always featured shrimp gumbo.

In 1951 Lawrence's oldest son, Lawrence Puccetti Jr., and his wife, Melba, took over the tavern and restaurant. Stern but caring, Puccetti soon endeared himself to the many medical students from the University of Texas Medical Branch who frequented the place. Though Puccetti adhered to his "no profanity" rule to the point where some rowdy customers got booted out, he also encouraged his young patrons and listened anytime they needed a friend. Thursday nights were especially busy when students came to study and eat. In 1996, as a token of their deep appreciation, two Austin physicians (both UTMB graduates)—Dr. Pierre Filardi and Dr. Byron Neely—established the Junior Puccetti Scholarship Fund. In turn, Puccetti throughout the years has honored students of long-time, continued attendance at Sonny's by engraving their names on small plaques, which hang on the restaurant walls. One in particular hails a student who visited Sonny's more than 800 consecutive days.

Besides the legendary plaques and an abundance of university memorabilia, the great food that Theresa once cooked still graces the table tops and booths at Sonny's. Fridays still feature shrimp gumbo, and muffulettas still reign as a top seller. Other menu favorites are shrimp buns, Theresa's spaghetti and meat sauce, the artery clogger (a chicken-fried steak sandwich with ranch dressing, cheeses, and vegetables), and a Coney Island hot dog.

What's a muffuletta, you're asking? It's a sandwich that originated in New Orleans in 1906. The key ingredients are crusty Italian bread and olive salad. Sonny's muffulettas are layered with ham, salami, mortadella (another kind of deli meat), provolone cheese, Swiss cheese, and Theresa's olive salad.

And oh, yes, folks also ask to see the infamous bullet hole in the bar. It was left there by an old-time hold-up. That HAD to have been before the Puccettis implemented their strict "behave or be gone!" policy, don't you think?

Gettin' there: From Highway 87, turn south on 19th Street.

Sonny's Place
1206 19th St.
Galveston, TX 77550

409/763-9602

Tex-Mex Pasta

pasta, your choice
chili, preferably homemade
American cheese
white cheese, your choice (Provolone, Parmesan, etc.)
corn tortillas
chopped onions, tomatoes, jalapeños
vegetable oil

Place a layer of white cheese on a plate. Then the amount of pasta you want, usually enough for one. Cover this with chili, then American cheese. Top with chopped vegetables. Cook until cheese melts. Fry and quarter corn tortillas; place around the outside of the plate.

Houston

Christie's Seafood & Steaks Restaurant (1917)

Love fish and shrimp? Head for Christie's. They've been cooking up some of the best for more than eighty years.

Christie's goes back to 1917 when Theodore Christie, a native of Istanbul, Turkey, opened a waterfront food and drink stand in Galveston. At his customers' request, he developed a "trout sandwich." The fried fish (the ancestor of today's modern fish stick) on a hoagie roll became an instant hit. In 1939 he moved his business to the Medical Center in Houston. On opening day he sold 2,000 of his trout sandwiches. Soon he was selling 10,000 a week!

Besides the fish stick, Christie is credited with creating the first seafood platter. At his restaurant, Christie served a variety of seafood on one dish and called it Christie's Fisherman's Platter.

After Christie died, his adopted son, Jim Christie, and a cousin, Steve Christie, became partners in the restaurant. They later split, and Steve, who opened other Christie's locations, retired in the early nineties. The Christie's on Westheimer, which is run by Jim and his family, is the only surviving restaurant.

To this day, Christie's still serves Theodore's popular trout sandwich. Though best known for fried shrimp and seafood, the restaurant also serves a variety of other dishes, such as Snapper Beluche (a recipe created by Jim), Snapper Opelousas (blackened fillet with shrimp, crab, mushrooms and green onion in a Cajun sauce); and Oysters Thermidor (sauteed oysters with crab in a light wine cream sauce with melted cheddar).

For those who need a Christie's fix but don't have time to sit down, there's a drive-in window for to-go orders.

Gettin' there: Christie's is located 1.5 miles west of the Galleria on Westheimer between Hillcroft and Fountainview Streets.

Christie's Seafood & Steaks Restaurant
6029 Westheimer Rd.
Houston, TX 77057
713/978-6563

Christie's Potatoes

2 ounces each: butter and flour (about ¼ cup each)
2 cups each: water and canned evaporated milk
1 tablespoon chicken bouillon granules
10 ounces mild cheddar cheese, grated, plus additional for garnish
4 large (about 10 ounces) freshly baked or boiled potatoes, peeled and diced in large squares

Melt butter and whisk in flour until smooth and the consistency of a light roux; do not brown. Set aside.

Bring water, milk, and chicken bouillon to a boil in a medium saucepan; whisk in grated cheese. When incorporated, whisk in roux. Combine sauce and potatoes in large (3-quart) baking dish. Sprinkle more cheese on top as desired and bake at 350 degrees until cheese melts and dish is bubbly. Makes 8 servings.

Christie's Snapper Beluche

4 8-ounce snapper fillets
salt and pepper to taste
vegetable oil
flour for dredging fish plus $\frac{1}{3}$ cup, divided
$\frac{1}{3}$ cup lightly salted butter plus 1 tablespoon, divided
2 cups water
1 teaspoon seafood bouillon granules
$\frac{1}{2}$ teaspoon chicken bouillon granules
8 slices Swiss cheese
1 cup whipping cream
$\frac{1}{3}$ teaspoon white pepper
$\frac{1}{4}$ cup cooking sherry (salted sherry)
12 medium shrimp, peeled and cleaned
1 cup sliced fresh mushrooms
$\frac{1}{3}$ cup chopped green onions or chives
8 ounces lump crab meat

Rinse fillets and pat dry. Season with salt and pepper. Heat just enough oil in a nonstick skillet to keep fish from sticking. Dredge fillets lightly in flour and arrange in pan. Sauté over medium-high heat, turning twice, until fish flakes easily, about 5 to 7 minutes.

Melt $\frac{1}{3}$ cup butter and whisk in $\frac{1}{3}$ cup flour. Stir until smooth, but do not let roux mixture brown. Set aside and keep warm. Bring water, seafood, and chicken bouillon granules to a boil. Add Swiss cheese slices and stir until melted and incorporated. Whisk in cream and add white pepper. Add warm roux mixture, whisking until well blended, smooth and thickened; whisk in sherry.

In large sauté pan, melt remaining 1 tablespoon butter and cook shrimp until half done. Add mushrooms and green onion. Sauté until mushrooms are tender. Add crab. Add cream mixture and bring to a boil; boil 1 minute. Portion over snapper fillets and serve immediately. Serves 4.

Felix Mexican Restaurant
(1929)

A Houston institution—that's what a lot of folks around town call the Felix. It's been around so long that what else could it be?

The story behind the Felix Mexican Restaurant starts with a young couple, struggling to make ends meet. Back in the 1930s Janie and Felix Tijerina lived in a sparse, one-room house in Houston. She worked at a variety store, and he drove a beer truck. One day Janie's boss gave her $50 to bet on a horse at Epsom Downs, a horse track near Houston that has since closed. Knowing her tightwad boss wouldn't risk parting with that much money unless he knew he had a sure thing, Janie—who had promised her husband that she wouldn't gamble any more—decided to bet on the same horse. But she wasn't going to plunk down a mere $50. Going for all she could, she pawned her jewelry, her furs, even the car she and Felix shared. She also gathered up a few dollars from her co-workers. In all, she bet $450.

And the horse won.

"Janie, what have you done?" asked a shocked Felix.

She confessed, then handed him $1,100, the leftover from her winnings (remember, she had to buy back their belongings). Use it to start your own restaurant, she told him.

And he did.

The Tijerinas' story is told in the March 11, 1997, Congressional Record, where Rep. Ken Bentsen of Houston asked to honor the memory of Janie after her death March 2 of the same year.

Felix Tijerina Sr., who died in 1965, was just as loved as his wife. Says his son, Felix Jr., "Dad felt real strongly that you should give back to the community so he always did what he could. He was especially involved with education. Felix Tijerina Elementary School on Sherman Street is named for my father."

According to Felix Jr., who runs the Felix with his family, the restaurant still serves basically the same menu his parents did. To keep up with the times, the Felix added fajitas and margaritas. Original menu items include the Felix Mexican Dinner, which—alas—doesn't cost 50 cents any more. But there ARE two from which to choose now. Number 1 dishes up one of each: a beef taco, tostada, tamale, and cheese enchilada, all served with Spanish rice or spaghetti. Number 2 features a beef taco, a tostada, and two cheese enchiladas. The Deluxe Dinner, then and now, piles on all the previously mentioned fare plus guacamole, chile con queso, rice or spaghetti, refried beans, tortillas, Mexican candy, and tea.

In 1999 a fire devastated the Felix. But the family persevered and reopened the beloved restaurant a little more than four months later...much to the relief of many folks around Houston who consider the Felix to be, well...a local institution.

Gettin' there: The Felix is located near the corner of Westheimer and Montrose not far from downtown.

Felix Mexican Restaurant
904 Westheimer Rd.
Houston, TX 77006
713/529-3949

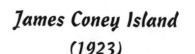

James Coney Island
(1923)

Who'd have thought a hot dog place would keep Houstonians coming for more than seven decades? Well, James Coney Island has, and the chain of restaurants is still going strong.

The popular eateries got their start when James and Tom Papadakis immigrated in the early 1900s from Greece to New York. There they ate a newfangled sandwich called a "Coney Island," better known today as the humble hot dog. The brothers separated awhile, then reconnected in Houston, where they decided to go into business together. But what should they name their new venture? The pair tossed a coin, and, well, you guessed it . . . James won.

The first James Coney Island opened in 1923 on Rusk Street. Three years later, they moved to the famous Walker Street location. Today, there are twenty-three James Coney Island eateries across Houston.

Annually, James Coney Island cooks up more than 7.5 million hot dogs! Customers order them plain or in a variety of other variations—with chili sauce and onions, Texas-style with chili, cheese, onions, and jalapeños, or New York-style with mustard and sauerkraut. The restaurants also serve their famous chili with beans and with or without Fritos. Burgers and a few sandwiches are also on the menu along with corn dogs, a tamale plate, and baked potatoes.

In case you're wondering, sausage and wieners have been around for centuries. The modern hot dog on a bun, hot dog historians believe, was invented in 1904 by Bavarian concessionaire Anton Feuchtwanger, who loaned white gloves to his customers so they could hold their hot sausages and not get messy. When he started running low on gloves, he asked his brother-in-law, a baker, for help. The ingenious in-law shaped and baked long, soft rolls that fit the sausage links. And—voila!—the hot dog bun was born.

Gettin' there: Pick one. They're all over town.

James Coney Island (1923)
5745 Westheimer
Houston, TX 77057
713/785-9333

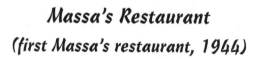

Massa's Restaurant
(first Massa's restaurant, 1944)

The story behind Massa's Restaurant on Smith Street in downtown Houston reads like a family saga. It begins with Michael Angelo Massa, a Sicilian immigrant who opened an oyster parlor in Galveston in 1900. The popular eatery served customers on the first floor. Upstairs, Michael lived with his wife and their nine children. In 1918, while visiting his homeland, Michael became sick and died.

In 1944 Tony Massa, one of Michael's sons, decided to set his sights on the booming Houston market and opened Massa's Oyster House, a restaurant specializing in seafood and steaks. Louis Massa, Tony's brother, later joined the business and opened two more Houston restaurants—the Rex Cafe and Massa's Cafeteria and Restaurant.

In 1981 Louis' sons, Michael and Joseph Massa, took over the family business. Today, the brothers each oversee their own restaurant. Michael runs the well-established Massa's Restaurant on Smith Street while Joseph manages the newer Massa's Seafood Grill on Lamar. Both establishments serve "contemporary Texas creole" cuisine in very upscale settings.

Professionally trained chefs create culinary masterpieces that look almost too beautiful to eat. Even the menu listings sound classy—grilled mango marinated shrimp, pumpkin-seed crusted rainbow trout, seafood quesadillas with creme Fraiche and pico de gallo, and barbecue salmon with spinach and arugula. The favorite Gulf fried shrimp, butterflied and breaded with seasoned crumbs, comes with jicama slaw, steak fries, and an onion ring.

Gettin' there: Massa's is located at the corner of Smith and Lamar Streets in downtown Houston.

Massa's Restaurant
1160 Smith St.
Houston, Tx 77002
713/650-0837

Stop by and see: You have to see to believe the Orange Show at 2402 Munger St. Impossible to describe, the incredible place was started in the 1950s by a Houston man obsessed with orange—both the fruit and the color.

Crawfish Cakes

½ cup chopped celery
½ cup chopped yellow onion
¼ cup chopped green onions
1 tablespoon chopped garlic
½ cup butter
1 pound crawfish tails, slightly chopped
1 cup cracker meal
¼ cup cilantro, chopped
2 eggs, beaten
salt and pepper
Tabasco

Saute vegetables and mix in other ingredients. Mold into cakes, approximately 2 to 4 ounces each. Lightly bread in cracker crumbs and saute over medium heat, about 3 minutes per side. Makes 12 servings.

Mango/Bourbon BBQ Sauce

1 tablespoon vegetable oil
1 onion, minced
½ cup roasted garlic, minced
1 pint ketchup
8 ounces chicken stock
8 ounces mango puree
4 ounces apple cider vinegar
2 ounces bourbon
3 ancho chiles, steamed, seeded, chopped
2 tablespoons brown sugar
2 tablespoons lemon juice

½ tablespoon BBQ spice
½ teaspoon black pepper, freshly ground
dash cayenne

Heat oil over medium heat. Add onions and garlic; saute until translucent. Add rest of ingredients and simmer for one hour; blend well. Makes 20 servings.

Jamie's Caesar Salad Dressing

2 egg yolks
3 tablespoons yellow mustard
2 tablespoons lemon juice
1 ½ teaspoons white wine vinegar
3 tablespoons capers, rinsed and drained
1 ½ teaspoon chopped garlic
4 tablespoons anchovies, rinsed and drained
2 tablespoons black pepper, freshly ground
2 cups olive oil
⅓ cup Parmesan cheese, grated
dash Tabasco

In a food processor, place yolks, mustard, garlic, anchovies, and capers. Process on low speed. Pour oil through hole in a slow, steady stream to emulsify into the mixture. When all of the oil is incorporated, add lemon juice and vinegar. If the mixture is too thick, add 1 or 2 tablespoons of water to thin. Finish dressing with Parmesan cheese and Tabasco.

Mango Vinaigrette

1 cup fresh mango, cubed
¼ cup white wine vinegar
1 ½ cups olive oil
1 teaspoon Tabasco
3 tablespoons cilantro, chopped
salt and pepper

Place mango, vinegar, and Tabasco in blender. Mix until pureed. Emulsify the olive oil into the mango mix. Finish with cilantro, salt, and pepper. Makes 8 servings.

Pino's Italian Restaurant
(1960)

Folks who've lived a long time in Houston remember Pino's Italian Restaurant on Cullen Boulevard. So is the Pino's on Hillcroft Street one and the same? The family gets asked that question almost on a daily basis. And the answer is YES!

The restaurant's story begins with Giuseppe "Pino" Fortunato Farinola, one of twelve children born to a couple in Brindisi, Italy. As a child, Pino worked in his father's small cafe, the Ristorante Moderno. In 1950 Pino and his brothers opened the Ristorante delle Nazione on the waterfront of Brindisi's port. The 300-seat restaurant quickly became popular with tourists and locals alike.

In 1958 Pino boarded an ocean liner and headed for America, where he planned to pursue his dreams in the "land of opportunity." He settled in Houston and worked as a cook at a nearby restaurant. It wasn't long before he landed a job as manager at another restaurant. After the business closed in the evenings, Pino mass produced his homemade cannelloni and lasagna. From the trunk of his car, he sold it to other restaurants. The Italian dishes were a hit, and pretty soon Pino had a thriving business of his own.

Lady luck smiled on Pino again in 1960 when he met a beautiful young woman by the name of Lenora Dayhoff. The couple fell instantly in love and married in less than three weeks. Two months later, using his savings and some borrowed funds, Pino and Lenora opened Pino's Italian Restaurant in an old two-bedroom house on Cullen Boulevard. Students from the nearby University of Houston became faithful customers of the restaurant, where they could enjoy a home-cooked meal for about two bucks. In 1970 the Farinola family moved Pino's Italian restaurant to its present two-story location on Hillcroft Street.

The popular eatery has a few claims to fame. "Our fresh, traditional food is prepared in a kitchen that has been voted the cleanest in Houston many times by both the Department of Health and Human Services and Channel 13," says the restaurant's website. Pino's has also garnered the most Marvin Zindler "Blue Ribbon Action Awards" for kitchen excellence. Fourteen, to be exact. The well-known television personality, who frequents Pino's at least once a week, reviews the city health inspector's reports on a weekly basis. Those restaurants that stay clean all year and do not appear on Marvin's televised reports win his "Blue Ribbon Action Awards," which are considered to be quite an accomplishment in Houston.

As for the food at Pino's, you won't find more Italian fare anywhere else. More than 60 items on the menu include lasagna, spaghetti and meatballs, linguine with clams, fish or Italian sausage, baked cheese ziti, fettuccine Alfredo, ravioli and tortellini, pizza, chicken Parmesan, chicken piccata, shrimp garlette, veal Parmesan, rib eye, and lamb. Children can choose from spaghetti and meatballs, fettuccine Alfredo, meat tortellini, or pizza.

And by the way, what's upstairs at Pino's? "That's another one of our most frequent questions," says the website. "Contrary to popular myth, there is not a disco or a private party room up there, although there might be someday. And no, it's not the secret residence of Pino. It's just a huge attic."

Inquiring minds always want to know.

Gettin' there: Pino's is located at the southeast corner of Westheimer and Hillcroft, west of the Galleria on Westheimer.

Pino's Italian Restaurant
2711 Hillcroft St.
Houston, TX 77057
713/783-2232
Website: www.pinosrestaurant.com

Huntsville

Cafe Texan
(1936)

Two steaks built Cafe Texan's long-lived reputation— chicken-fried and peppered. Folks come from all over to eat one or the other at the venerable downtown restaurant. Fred Morris opened the cafe in 1936 and sold peppered fried steaks for a bargain 36 cents. He's been gone since 1958, but the cafe still serves his specialty—grilled steaks simmered au jus with whole black peppercorns. As for the crispy chicken-fries, customers wolf down more than 5,000 a month of those.

Not much has changed at the Texan, often called the "Cowboy Headquarters of Huntsville." A pressed-tin ceiling hovers above the dining room's sixteen counter stools and scarred tables, most of which are original.

On the cover, the menu politely advises customers that Cafe Texan is not a fast-food place and that lunch plates—

prepared on a by-customer basis—can take as long as a half hour to arrive.

"We do appreciate your business, but if you need something fast, we suggest you try one of the other fine establishments in Huntsville," the menu reads.

Most folks prefer the wait.

Gettin' there: From I-45, take Texas 30 Exit East. Go to the courthouse intersection of Texas 30 and Sam Houston Avenue. The Texan is across from the courthouse at 1120 Sam Houston Ave.

Cafe Texan
1120 Sam Houston
Huntsville, TX 77340
409/295-2381

Stop by and see: The Texas Prison Museum on 12th Street . . . OK, it's not a real cheerful place to visit. But you'll see lots of interesting exhibits, like old ball-and-chains and rifles used by Bonnie and Clyde.

Jefferson

Club Cafe
(1920s)

The owners have changed several times, and the location has moved once. But for more than 60 years, the Club Cafe has fed folks around Jefferson. You won't find fancy food here nor a whole lot to choose from on the menu, but the prices are reasonable and the atmosphere definitely down home. So down home and small town that a few scenes from the 1988 film *Big Bad John* (starring Jimmy Dean and Jack Elam) were shot inside and out of the cafe.

The Club Cafe's decor, which isn't fancy either, fits the classic cafe style. Plastic tablecloths cover the square tables that each seat four. Waitresses busily work behind a counter area, equipped with a coffee machine, ice machine, refrigerator, and shelves lined with plastic glasses, coffee mugs, and water pitchers. Customers show up by six in the morning, when breakfast starts. Four bucks buys a "Country Breakfast," complete with two eggs, bacon or sausage, and two hot cakes. The menu also offers omelettes, French toast, biscuits, and sweet rolls. At noon, the Club Cafe serves burgers, sandwiches, lunch baskets (chicken fingers, steak fingers, catfish nuggets, and shrimp), salads, and soup.

Gettin' there: From Interstate 20 East or West, take the Marshall Exit, U.S. 59 north. Travel about 15 miles north to the first Jefferson exit (Business 59). Road runs straight for about 2 miles, then splits. Bear left. This brings you right into downtown Jefferson. At the first stop light, Club Cafe is on the left.

Club Cafe
109 N. Polk St.
Jefferson, TX 75657
903/665-2881

Stop by and see: Jefferson is another one of those quaint Texas towns that's fun to explore. Lots of antique shops, great restaurants, historic homes, romantic bed-and-breakfasts, and beautiful churches make Jefferson a great weekend get-away, too.

Chicken and Dumplings

3 pounds chicken
10 cups water
4 cups flour
½ teaspoon salt
½ cup margarine
1 cup milk
2 eggs
3 tablespoons chicken base or bouillon

Bring water and chicken to a boil, and simmer until done. Mix flour, salt, margarine, milk, and eggs together in medium-sized bowl. Divide the dough in thirds. Roll one third on a floured surface to ⅛ inches thick. With a sharp knife, cut strips 1-inch wide and 2 inches long. Set the pieces on a floured tray and set aside. Continue with the next third of dough until all is cut into pieces.

When the chicken is done, spoon meat out of water and set aside to cool. Add the chicken base to the water and bring back to boil. When water is at a rapid boil, add dumplings and simmer until done, about 15 to 20 minutes.

Remove chicken from the bones and put into a serving pan. When dumplings are done, add them to the chicken and thicken the chicken broth. Pour the thickened gravy over the chicken and dumplings until everything mixes well and is not dry (you may use all of the gravy). Makes 15 one-and-a-half cup servings.

Chicken and Wild Rice Soup

8 cups water
1½ cups chicken, cooked and cubed
½ cup wild rice
¼ cup white rice
salt and pepper to taste
parsley

Bring water to a boil and add cubed chicken, pepper, salt, and wild rice. Simmer until rice is almost done, about 40 minutes. Add the white rice, simmer until done. Add parsley. Makes about 10 one-cup servings.

Longview

Johnny Cace's Seafood & Steak House
(1949)

A cardboard sign hanging near the front entrance of Johnny Cace's Seafood & Steak House bears this thoughtful motto— "Succcess is never final. Failure is never fatal. It's courage that counts."

Johnny Cace Jr. has lived his long life in step with that framed slogan. He's taken chances and never given up. His reward: customers still faithfully frequent his restaurant, Johnny Cace's Seafood & Steak House, more than a half century later.

Born in New Orleans in 1917, Cace worked for his father in an oyster camp and learned how to harvest oysters and catch fish. In 1935 his family moved to Shreveport and opened a seafood market there. In the family's seafood restaurant, young Cace honed his cooking skills, preparing gumbo and stuffed crabs Louisiana style. At the beginning of World War II, he volunteered to serve in the Air Force and worked four years as mess sergeant at Moore Field in McAllen. He married in 1939 and ten years later moved to Longview, where he opened his own seafood restaurant downtown. The small cafe seated 37 customers. At first, business waned, and Cace fretted. But not for long. He hung on, and it wasn't long before local ball players began stopping by after games for supper at the restaurant. Cace's worry soon gave way to astonishment and optimism. Johnny Cace's Seafood and Steak House was on its way to becoming an East Texas legend.

Since its start in 1949, the restaurant has moved once and expanded five times. Today, Johnny Cace's seats 450 guests and has a waiting area big enough to hold 150. And the menu . . . the number of delectable possibilities is almost overwhelming. Appetizers, for instance, include Crabmeat Pontchartrain, baked crabmeat topped with Newburg sauce and cheese. Oysters Casino are fresh oysters on the shell, baked with a cheese-and-wine sauce and sprinkled with bacon bits. For dinner, there's a number of different fish entrees, crawfish pasta, stuffed shrimp, stuffed crab, frog legs, and combinations thereof. Customers can also choose from lobster tail, rib eye steak, baked stuffed flounder, char-broiled tuna, and broiled salmon. One of the restaurant's trademark specialties is "Shrimp in Shorts," butterflied shrimp covered with a thin breading and deep fried.

Folks who've eaten at Johnny Cace's since childhood will certainly remember the popular "treasure chest," a regular fixture at the restaurant since it opened in 1949. After their meals, children 12 and under may pick out one treasure from the box, filled with trinkets and surprises.

Today, one of Cace's three sons, Gerard (and his wife, Cathy), run the Longview restaurant. His other two sons have restaurants of their own: John Cace III owns the Bayou Riverside Restaurant in San Antonio, and Danny Cace is the majority owner of Cace's Seafood in Tyler.

Gettin' there: Johnny Cace's is located on East Marshall Ave. (U.S. 80) in Longview just west of Eastman Road (U.S. 259).

Johnny Cace's Seafood & Steak House
1501 E. Marshall Ave.
Longview, TX 75601
903/753-7691

Other Cace locations:

Bayou Riverside Restaurant
(on the River Walk)
517 N. Presa St.
San Antonio, TX 78205
210/223-6403

Cace's Seafood
7011 S. Broadway Ave.
Tyler, TX 75703
903/581-0744

Paris

South Main Depot Restaurant
formerly the South Main Cafe (1934)

Folks in Paris used to buy groceries and meet for supper at the old South Main Cafe on Main Street. Clark Caviness built the original building in 1932 as a gas station. He and his wife lived upstairs until 1949 when they built a house next door. The couple sold the business in 1978 to new owners who kept the local landmark going. The gas station part of the business shut down in 1985, and the grocery store followed in 1990. Four years later, Robert and Irene Foreman took over the restaurant. In 1999 they moved the cafe into an 1887 train depot across the street and renamed it the South Main Depot Restaurant.

"We still serve the same good food with daily specials," Irene says. "The depot has a lot of charm and is a very popular place in Paris."

Speaking of daily specials, the most popular is meat loaf on Thursdays. Customers also love Wednesdays, designated as "chicken and dressing day." The Friday special features enchiladas.

The cafe is also famous for its homemade rolls and Irene's delicious cream pies—coconut, chocolate, lemon, banana cream, and pineapple.

Gettin' there: Paris is 103 miles northeast of Dallas.

South Main Cafe
1264 S. Main St.
Paris, TX 75460
903/785-3400

Stop by and see: The Sam Bell Maxey State Historic Structure at 812 S. Church Street was built in 1868 by Confederate general Maxey. The Maxey family lived in the Victorian-style, two-story home for nearly a century.

Chicken Salad

Boil two fryer chickens. Debone and cut into medium-sized pieces. Dice desired amount of celery and walnuts. Mix into chicken with a pinch of salt and 2-3 tablespoons of sugar and salad dressing (adjust as wanted to desired consistency).

Bread Pudding

2 loaves bread
$\frac{1}{2}$ gallon milk
3 cups sugar
4 eggs
2 tablespoons nutmeg

Dissolve bread in milk. Add remaining ingredients. Bake for an hour and a half at 275 degrees. Serve with warm vanilla sauce.

Vanilla sauce:
1 teaspoon vanilla
$\frac{1}{2}$ teaspoon cinnamon
$\frac{1}{4}$ cup cornstarch
1 $\frac{1}{2}$ cups sugar
2 cups milk

Mix and cook over low heat until thickened.

Spring

Wunsche Bros. Cafe & Saloon
(1902)

Much like the quaint towns of Salado and Fredericksburg, Old Town Spring is a fun place to spend a day shopping and dining. People come from nearby Houston and even farther away to stroll the tree-lined streets and browse through the many stores housed in wood-framed cottages.

Spring sprang up back in 1838 when William Pierpont established a trading post along Spring Creek. Two years later, the community boasted 153 residents. In 1871 the Houston and Great Northern Railroad came through town and triggered a boom. By the early 1880s the town had two steam saw- and gristmills, two cotton gins, three churches, and several schools.

In 1902 brothers Dell, Charlie, and William Wunsche, descendants of Spring's early German farming families, saw the lucrative potential of a new roundhouse (a circular structure for housing and switching locomotives) and a branch rail line extending west. So they built the town's first two-story building, made from longleaf pine cut at their own sawmill, near the depot and tracks. The Wunsche Bros. Hotel and Saloon accommodated railroad employees traveling up and down the Galveston-Houston-Palestine line. Within a year what is now Old Town Spring had five hotels, five saloons, a hospital, and an opera house. Prosperity had come to Spring, which had become a major switchyard with 14 track yards and 200 rail workers.

The rip roaring times lasted until Prohibition came along in 1920. Then in 1923 Houston and Great Northern moved the Spring rail yard to Houston. By 1926 most of the town's buildings were scrapped for barn and firewood. Economic activity in

Spring dwindled to almost nothing. But thanks to hamburgers, the town did survive.

In 1949 Viola Burke leased the Wunsche building and renamed it the "Spring Cafe." She started cooking homemade burgers for railroad workers still passing through town. The big, juicy sandwiches were an instant hit, and soon folks from clear across the county came to eat Viola's hamburgers. When she died in 1976, daughter Irma Ansley inherited the business and continued her mother's legacy. In the early seventies lines for a burger at the Spring Cafe grew long. One resourceful couple, seeing a lucrative opportunity (like the Wunsche brothers did in 1902), opened a gift shop for cafe customers so they could kill time while they waited for a table. One by one, more shops opened, and Spring became the charming retail attraction that it is today. More than 80 specialty shops line the streets!

In 1982 Brenda and Scott Mitchell bought the building from the Wunsche family. After six months of extensive renovation, the couple opened the Wunsche Bros Cafe & Saloon.

"What makes our menu special is that is satisfies Texas cafe standards, yet takes our customers beyond their expectations of ordinary cafe food," writes Brenda in the *Wunsche Bros. Cafe Cookbook*, which she published in 1993. "Down-home specials like chicken 'n' dumplings, jambalaya, and fried catfish are offered next to unexpected originals like Pasta Santa Fe and Sausage Crumb Salad."

At the Wunsche Bros. Cafe, everything's prepared fresh and from scratch. On the menu (more like a tabloid newspaper you can take home), a bushel of appetizer and vegetable selections include black bean and corn salsa, beer bread, the cafe's famous sausage sauerkraut balls (recipe follows), squash casserole, and stewed okra and tomatoes. "Main" attractions—naturally—feature the whopping Wunsche Burger, a half-pounder with the works. There's also Cajun-grilled catfish, chicken-fried steak, char-grilled chicken salad, and a German sausage sandwich. And in case you're wondering what's a Sausage Crumb Salad, that's a large garden salad with sauerkraut balls crumbled over the top and served with beer bread. For dessert, try a slice of Brenda's intoxicatingly good Chocolate Whiskey Cake, a dark chocolate delight with pecans and a little kick. Oreo cheesecake topped with fudge sauce and chocolate amaretto cream pie taste pretty darn good, too.

If you don't have room for dessert, take a stroll around Old Town Spring. Then come on back. Wunsche Bros. Cafe & Saloon stays open late (except Mondays).

Gettin' there: Old Town Spring is a 10-square-block shopping district that lies about 20 miles north of downtown Houston. From I-45 take exit 70A, go east one mile on Spring-Cypress Road, and take either road at the Y. Both lead to Spring's primary shopping streets.

Wunsche Bros. Cafe & Saloon
103 Midway St.
Spring, TX 77383
281/350-1902

The following recipes are excerpted from the *Wunsche Bros. Cafe Cookbook*.

Hands down, Brenda says, this is the cafe's most talked about food. "People come here from all over the country and tell us they've heard about our sauerkraut balls," she writes in her cookbook. "I love to hear a customer say, 'Oh, I don't like sauerkraut.' They are the very ones who end up raving about these and coming back for more."

Sausage Sauerkraut Balls

1 pound bulk sausage
1½ cups grated mild cheddar cheese
3 eggs
1 cup sauerkraut, drained and squeezed dry
1 small onion, chopped
dried bread crumbs
beer batter (recipe follows)

Mix all ingredients by hand. (Try not to break sauerkraut strands.) Shape into 1- to 1½-inch balls and roll in bread crumbs. Refrigerate until ready to deep fry. When ready to fry, dip in beer batter and deep fry in 375-degree oil until golden brown. Serve with sour cream chive dip.

Beer Batter

2 cups all-purpose flour
1 teaspoon baking powder
1 tablespoon salt
1 ½ cups beer
1 ½ teaspoons garlic powder
oil for deep frying

Combine flour, salt, garlic powder, and baking powder in a bowl. Add beer and whisk until smooth. Cover and chill 30 minutes. Whisk again, then let stand in refrigerator until ready to use. Batter can be prepared one day ahead, if desired.

Pasta Santa Fe is a very popular dish at Wunsche Bros., Brenda says. Since this recipe requires many steps, you might prepare part of the dish the day before serving. Read the entire recipe before beginning.

Pasta Santa Fe

2 pounds spaghetti
8 chicken breasts, skinned and deboned, marinated (recipe follows)
2 green bell peppers, halved and seeded
2 yellow bell peppers, halved and seeded
1 cup cilantro, finely chopped
1 cup sliced black olives
Salsa Vinaigrette (recipe follows)

Prepare Salsa Vinaigrette. Prepare Chicken Marinade and marinate chicken. Grill chicken breasts. Grill pepper halves until charred black and blistered. Place pepper halves in a bowl and cover with plastic wrap until cool. Remove and peel blistered skin.

Cook spaghetti in boiling water according to directions on package. While spaghetti is cooking, cut chicken breasts and peppers into long strips. In a sauce pan, heat Salsa Vinaigrette until just warm. Drain spaghetti and put in a large bowl. Toss Salsa Vinaigrette with spaghetti. Add chicken strips, pepper strips, black olives, and cilantro; toss lightly. Serve warm.

Chicken Marinade

2 tablespoons soy sauce
1/4 cup chardonnay wine
I tablespoon dried tarragon
1/2 teaspoon salt
1/2 tablespoon garlic powder
3/4 cup margarine, melted

Combine all ingredients and marinate chicken at least 2 hours.

Salsa Vinaigrette

I cup olive oil
I cup safflower oil
3/4 cup white wine vinegar
3 tablespoons Dijon mustard
4 cups Salsa (recipe follows)

Blend oils and vinegar; whisk in mustard. Mix 3 cups vinaigrette to 4 cups salsa.

Salsa

3 tomatoes, diced
I cup green onions, chopped
I jalapeño pepper, minced
I tablespoon cilantro, minced
I tablespoon fresh lemon juice
2 cups canned whole tomatoes with juice, cut into chunks
I cup mild Pace picante sauce

Combine all ingredients in a bowl. Cover and refrigerate 8 to 10 hours.

This is Brenda's very favorite coffee cake.

Spicy Buttermilk Coffee Cake

2 1/4 cups flour
3/4 cup corn oil
1/2 teaspoon salt
2 teaspoons cinnamon
I cup walnuts or pecans, chopped
1/4 teaspoon ginger

1 teaspoon baking soda
1 cup brown sugar
1 teaspoon baking powder
¾ cup white sugar
1 egg, beaten
1 cup buttermilk

Step 1: Make the batter and topping mix. Mix together in a large bowl the flour, salt, 1 teaspoon of the cinnamon, ginger, both sugars, and corn oil. Remove ¾ cup of this mixture, and to it add walnuts or pecans and an additional teaspoon cinnamon. Mix well and set aside.

Step 2: Complete the batter. To the remaining batter, add baking soda, baking powder, egg, and buttermilk. Mix to combine all ingredients.(Small lumps in the batter are OK.)

Step 3: Bake. Pour batter into a well-greased 9x13x2-inch pan. Sprinkle the topping mixture evenly over the surface. Bake at 350 degrees for 40 to 45 minutes.

A simple but utterly delicious peanut butter cookie, Brenda says. It was originally given to her by the cafe's first baker, Donna Bond, who now owns her own bakery.

Peanut Butter Cookies

½ cup butter
½ cup granulated sugar
½ cup light brown sugar
½ cup crunchy peanut butter
1 egg
½ teaspoon vanilla
1¼ cups flour
¾ teaspoon soda
¼ teaspoon salt

Cream butter with sugars; add peanut butter. Beat in egg and vanilla. Sift the flour with the baking soda and salt; fold into batter mixture. Shape dough into 1-inch balls. Place 2 inches apart on cookie sheet. Flatten slightly with a fork, using crisscross pattern. Bake at 350 degrees for 10 to 12 minutes or until cookies are lightly brown.

> ### Texas Historical Marker Wunsche Bros. Saloon and Hotel
>
> This building was constructed in 1902 by one of Spring's earliest families, the Wunsches, who came here from Germany in 1846. Built to accommodate railroad workers, the Wunsche Bros. Saloon and Hotel, later known as the Spring Cafe, has served as a community gathering place throughout its history. The structure, which exhibits typical turn-of-the-century commercial detailing, is Spring's oldest existing commercial building on its original site.

Tomball

Goodson's Cafe

(1950)

Right place, right time. That coupled with experience and know-how paved the way for Ella Goodson when she took over a small cafe near Tomball in the early fifties.

She'd only worked there four years when the owner decided to sell. He convinced Ella that she should buy it, and she did—just at the right time. The oil fields around Tomball were booming with activity, and roughnecks by the dozens crowded into "Ma" Goodson's restaurant to eat. Word got around about her cooking talents, and local folks began to frequent the cafe, too. Many ordered Ma's chicken-fried steak, her trademark specialty. Pretty soon, Houstonians drove to Tomball solely to dine at Goodson's Cafe, and business executives even flew in by helicopter.

Through the years, Ma and her CFS gained even more attention. The cafe's been featured several times on *The Eyes of Texas* television show, which proclaimed Ma's CFS "the Best in Texas." In 1992 *Texas Highways*' readers also lauded her CFS.

Though Ma has since retired, her famous chicken-fried steak, served with homemade cream gravy, vegetables, and yeast rolls, still ropes in customers from far and wide. For folks with different tastes, Goodson's also serves a selection of chicken entrees, pork chops, ribs, steaks, seafood, salads, and burgers.

Likely lots of Houston folks couldn't have been happier when Goodson's opened a second location in their town. The cafe, located on North Gessner Drive, seats more than 180 people, and—wonder of wonders—it serves chicken-fried steak fixed just the way Ma used to make it.

But the favorite place to cut into her gravy-kissed CFS will always be the original Goodson's Cafe in Tomball.

Gettin' there: Goodson's Cafe is located 10 miles north of FM 196 on Tomball Parkway.

Goodson's Cafe
27931 Tomball Pkwy.
Tomball, TX 77375
281/351-1749

Second location:
Goodson's Cafe
1045 Gessner Dr.
Houston, TX 77055
713/973-2233

Stop by and see: The Community Museum Center at 510 N. Pine St. preserves twelve old structures that include a Victorian home, a mid-1800s farmhouse, a pioneer country doctor's office, and a one-room schoolhouse.

Waskom

New Waskom Cafe
(1928)

Interstate highways offer an efficient means of traversing the Lone Star State. But as you speed along the asphalt toward your destination, you also miss a lot of small-town Texas. Next time you're traveling east via Interstate 20, pull off before you get to the Louisiana border and visit Waskom. This little town of 1,900 residents has its own tried-and-true restaurant, the New Waskom Cafe. The local landmark, built around 1928, used to stay open 'round the clock to feed travelers on U.S. 80. But when the interstate opened in the mid-sixties, business slowed down, and the cafe cut back its hours.

Since it's been around so long, the New Waskom has plenty of history. For instance, back when it was open 24 hours a day, emergency calls for the local volunteer fire department used to be answered and dispatched through the restaurant. It also served as the local bus stop. But the most famous bit of history is the day the cafe turned around. Literally. It happened after the U.S. 80 route moved from the restaurant's north side to the south. Determined to keep their highway presence, the owners had the building hydraulically lifted and turned so it once again faced the road. During the lifting process, the cook never stopped working in the kitchen, and waitresses kept filling up customers' coffee cups.

Current owner Brenda Westbrook loves the lore and history that surround her business. In fact, her affection for the old cafe was so strong that she bought it in 1997, even though she had no restaurant experience. Determined to preserve the landmark, she immediately went to work on restoring the building to its 1950s appearance. She also filled the walls with old photographs of the area's past and present. "I'm trying to keep it as close to original as it used to be," Brenda says. And she has. "I've had people who haven't visited in 40 years come in and say, 'Oh, gosh, it looks just the same!'"

Old-time customers are also pleased to see that the New Waskom still serves "cackleberry" (slang for when a hen lays an egg and then cackles)—an egg with toast, homemade biscuits, and grits or hash browns. Daily lunch specials are popular, and so are the cafe's chicken-fried steak, open-face hot roast beef sandwiches, and old-fashioned hamburgers.

166

Speaking of old, one of the oldest pay phones still operates in the New Waskom Cafe. You can even still make a local call for a dime. Isn't that worth pulling off the interstate for?

Gettin' there: From I-20, take exit 635 to Waskom. The cafe is located on US 80, a half mile west of Spur 156.

New Waskom Cafe
260 E. Texas Ave.
Waskom, TX 75692
903/687-4028
Website: www.newwaskomcafe.com

Stop by and see: T.C. Lindsey & Co. is part old-fashioned store, part museum. Scenes from several Disney films have been shot here. Located 3 miles west of Waskom on FM 134.

Mama's Hot Water Corn Bread
$\frac{3}{4}$ cup cornmeal
$\frac{1}{2}$ cup flour
I teaspoon salt
I level teaspoon baking powder

In a saucepan, bring approximately I quart of water to a boil. Mix all the above ingredients. Slowly add boiling water to mixture (enough to make mixture moist). Form into patties after wetting hands in cold water so mixture will not

167

stick to hands. Drop into hot vegetable oil and cook until golden brown.

Brenda says this is an old family recipe she acquired in 1965.

Old-Fashioned Swiss Steak

I round steak

Sauce:
I can tomato sauce
¼ cup flour
I piece celery, chopped fine
¼ medium bell pepper
I small onion, chopped fine
I small button garlic (optional)

Cut steak in serving pieces. Flour, salt, and pepper steak and brown in small amount of shortening. Brown onions, celery, pepper, and garlic in fat from steak. Drain off fat in skillet, then add flour, tomato sauce, and 2 cups hot water. Cook in a 325-degree oven for 1½ hours.

This is a specialty at the New Waskom Cafe.

Old-Fashioned Coconut Pie

2 cups sugar
¼ cup cornstarch
4 eggs (separate and use yolks in pie and whites in meringue)
2½ cups milk
I tablespoon butter
¼ teaspoon salt
I teaspoon vanilla
I 10-inch pie shell, baked

Mix and boil ingredients until thick. Add coconut and stir until well mixed. Pour into the pie shell. For meringue topping, beat egg whites, adding about ¼ cup sugar and ¼ teaspoon cream of tartar. Spread on top of pie, sprinkle with coconut, then brown lightly in the oven at 350 degrees.

Other old-time restaurants:

Beaumont
Sartin's Seafood (1972)
6725 Eastex Freeway
Beaumont, TX 77709
409/892-6771

Brenham
Santa Fe and SP Cafe (1930s)
302 W. First St.
Brenham, TX 77833
409/836-0573

Caldwell
Jake's Restaurant (1956)
Highway 36
Caldwell, TX 77836
409/567-3797

College Station
Dixie Chicken (1974)
307 University Dr.
College Station, TX 77840
409/846-2322

Houston
Prince's Hamburgers
(1929 Dallas, 1934 Houston)
8808 Westheimer
Houston, TX 77063
713/334-1950

Zinnante's Delicatessen (1972)
9806 Hillcroft
Houston, TX 77096
713/723-7001

Marshall
Neely's Sandwich Shop (1927)
1404 E. Grand Ave.
Marshall, TX 75670
903/935-9040

Nederland
Nederland Lunch Counter (1920s)
1100 Boston Ave.
Nederland, TX 77627
409/729-3807

Tyler

Fuller's Fine Food (1950)
601 E. Front St.
Tyler, TX 75702
903/593-3572

Loggins Restaurant (1949)
137 S. Glenwood Blvd.
Tyler, TX 75702
903/595-5022

Westward, ho

Big Spring

Herman's Restaurant
(1960)

Herman's Restaurant has been around since 1960 when Herman Wilkerson greeted his first customers at the door. Herman had one son, Homer, who later took over the business with his wife, Stina.

"We've operated continuously since that date and still employ some of the original people who started with Herman way back then," Stina says.

Reliably good chicken-fried steak and luscious homemade yeast rolls bring the customers back. A few other traditions entice them, too. "Every Sunday, we have turkey and dressing," Stina says. "And the customers sure come and get it! They even stand in line for it. Plus, we make our mashed potatoes from real potatoes. We're just a real old-fashioned cafe that still serves old-fashioned plate lunches at noon. We have one entree, which changes daily. It might be chicken and dumplings, meat loaf, smothered steak, or fried chicken—whatever we decide to cook. Our dessert of the day is usually a fruit cobbler, banana, chocolate, or coconut pudding, or maybe a creamy rice pudding. Occasionally, we serve German chocolate or carrot cake."

"Our claim to fame is not a beautiful building but good, consistent food," Stina adds.

Gettin' there: Herman's is located between 16th and 17th Streets on Gregg Street, also called Highway 87.

Herman's Restaurant
1601 S. Gregg St.
Big Spring, TX 79720
915/267-3281

Stop by and see: Comanche Trail Park, south of town off U.S. 87, features a huge spring that gave Big Spring its name.

Fabens

Cattleman's Steakhouse
(1973)

Texans will drive out of their way for two things: a good steak and great seafood. Cattleman's Steakhouse south of El Paso has both, but the restaurant is much better known for its steaks.

How can a steak house located in the middle of nowhere be so successful? Owner Dieter Gerzymisch gets asked that question a lot. His story begins in 1966 when he was working for his father's shipping business in Germany, their homeland. "I was put in charge of moving the German Air Force School and its soldiers to Fort Bliss," he recalls. "Business brought me to Fort Bliss and El Paso again in 1968. The unique flavor and the friendly people made such an impression on me, that I decided to make it my home."

That same year, he bought several livery horses at historic Hueco Tanks east of El Paso and let a friend manage the horse-riding business. A few months later, however, El Paso County gave the site, which preserves ancient Indian rock art, to the Texas Parks and Wildlife Department, and it became a state park. In need of a new home for his horses, Dieter searched for property and found some ranch land near Fabens southeast of El Paso. In its new location at Indian Cliffs, the horse-riding business thrived. Three years later, Dieter realized his customers needed a place to eat. So in 1972 he started building a restaurant, and it opened the following year. Word spread about the steak house, and people came from miles away. When waiting lines became too long, Dieter decided to expand the restaurant, which he did in 1978.

Along the way, he also added more attractions at Indian Cliffs Ranch, which today includes numerous party facilities, a four-acre lake, horse corrals, and a snake pit. A small children's zoo features goats, mouflon sheep, llamas, fallow deer, rabbits, and prairie dogs. Fort Apache is a rustic children's playground with three wooden fort-like structures and a covered wagon. Fort Misery is a replica of an 1860s frontier fort complete with bunkhouse, a look-out tower, and a jail house. Several movies have been filmed at Fort Misery and around Indian Cliffs Ranch, including *Extreme Prejudice* with Nick Nolte, *Lone Wolf McQuade* with Chuck Norris, and *Courage Under Fire* with Denzel Washington and Meg Ryan.

Though Old West attractions abound at the ranch, most folks come for mesquite-charred steaks at Cattleman's Steak-house. The restaurant, which resembles a hacienda-style adobe ranch house, has won lots of accolades for serving the best steaks in the region. For instance, readers of *Texas Highways* magazine in '92 and '98 ranked Cattleman's among the state's top 10 restaurants. In '97 the restaurant captured six categories in the annual *El Paso Times* "Best of the Border" awards: best restaurant, romantic dinner, family-style dinner, brisket, steak, and margaritas.

Dinners at Cattleman's are served family style. Fixin's include baked potatoes, ranch beans, coleslaw, and baskets of bread. The biggest steak on the menu is The Cowboy, a 2-pound porterhouse T-bone. Smaller appetites can order the Little Wrangler, a 7-ounce sirloin steak, or the Lady's Filet, a 6-ounce cut. For those who prefer seafood, there's orange roughy, shrimp scampi, and lobster (on the menu, the latter is priced at a "king's ransom"), all steamed and served with hot butter on the side. For dessert, Cattleman's serves several temptations: homemade cheesecake, chocolate mousse, apple pie, and pecan pie.

The grand finale after supper is watching the sun set across the desert. Folks come from miles around just to see that, too.

Gettin' there: Cattleman's is located approximately 35 minutes from downtown El Paso. Take I-10 east and turn left at Fabens, Exit 49. Go 5 miles north into the desert.

Cattleman's Steakhouse
P.O. Box 1056
Fabens, TX 79838
915/544-3200
Website: www.cattlemanssteakhouse.com

Beef Stroganoff

2 pounds sirloin beef
1 cup beef broth
4 tablespoons butter
1 tablespoon flour
1 tablespoon mustard (regular or dijon style)
1 clove garlic
1 medium onion, diced
5 tablespoons sour cream
salt and pepper to taste

Trim fat and gristle from meat and cut into strips, about 1½ to 2 inches long by ½ inch thick. Season with salt and pepper. In a skillet or saucepan, melt 2 tablespoons butter; add flour and stir until blended. Heat the broth and add the butter-flour mixture to it, stirring until sauce is thickened and smooth, then add mustard. Heat the remaining butter in a skillet; add meat and onion, and brown all over. Remove meat from skillet to a plate and add sour cream to thickened mustard sauce. Heat until boiling, then pour over meat and serve. Serves about 6.

Fort Davis

Black Bear Restaurant

formerly the Restaurant at Indian Lodge (1935)

My family loves Indian Lodge. Every summer we rendezvous with my parents, load up a van (depending on whose turn it is to take theirs—mine or Dad's), and make the six-hour trip to Davis Mountain State Park in West Texas. We started the tradition in 1990 and have been going there ever since.

Over the years, lots of people have stayed at the pueblo-style hotel and eaten at the restaurant there. The Civilian Conservation Corps built the original 15 rooms and lobby building in the 1930s. The white exterior walls are more than 18 inches thick and made of adobe bricks molded on site. Cottonwood logs form ceiling beams, window frames, and doorframes. Heavy cedar furniture, constructed at Bastrop State Park by CCC workers, remains in use today in the lobby and in some of the original rooms. A restaurant in a lower room fed guests and local residents.

In 1967 the TPWD modernized the Indian Lodge and added two wings with 24 rooms, a swimming pool, a meeting facility, and a new dining room. The "new" guestrooms feature Indian-style furniture designed especially for the hotel. Some rooms open onto a central courtyard planted with native cacti, trees, and flowers. Others have spectacular views of Kessey Canyon and the mountains.

For five days, the Rodgers and the Smiths (that's my parents) hike the mountains, feed the birds, see the sights, swim in the lodge's pool, and eat at the Black Bear Restaurant. The cheerful waitresses, who know our faces well, always seem glad to see us every summer. After about the fifth day the menu gets a bit routine to us, but we manage somehow. We like being able to walk from our rooms straight to breakfast, lunch, and supper!

For more than five decades the restaurant didn't have a name. Folks just called it the Restaurant at Indian Lodge. In 1992 Mike Crevier with Texas Parks and Wildlife Department decided the dining room needed its own identity, and it became the Black Bear Restaurant.

Yes, there's a story behind the name. You knew there would be.

An outdated menu tells the tale. In the 1930s black bears freely roamed the Davis Mountains and occasionally preyed on livestock. One day a local rancher who was tracking bears found two abandoned cubs in a tree. One fell out of the branches and died. The other cub went home with the rancher, who raised the little female as a pet.

"Bear," as she was called, broke her chain one day and ambled over to the Prude Ranch where a group of CCC men were enjoying a Sunday outing. It wasn't long before they met Bear, who chased them up a windmill and kept them there until help arrived. While the men ventured down, someone else tried to rope Bear and accidentally hurt her. The CCC men, feeling bad about the ordeal, volunteered to take her back to the park and care for her. Bear went and became the camp's mascot. She regularly visited the men's tents at night and often "helped" during construction of Indian Lodge. She died in 1934 at the age of five.

Black bears have long since left the area. The last one was captured in 1963. The Black Bear Restaurant perpetuates the memory of their existence in the Davis Mountains. On the menu, however, you won't find bear steaks. Instead, breakfast fixings feature eggs, hash browns, pancakes, burritos, biscuits and gravy, and pastries. For lunch and dinner, there're sandwiches, chicken-fried steak, chopped steak with grilled onions, charbroiled rib eye, chicken picatta, fried catfish, enchiladas, and fajitas. A small soup and salad bar serves the daily soup (the tortilla soup on Wednesday is terrific), a big bowl of lettuce salad, and a few other cold salads, like green pea, potato, and Jell-O.

After a meal at the Black Bear, we Rodgers and Smiths engage in another family tradition—climb a rocky mountain trail and burn off the extra calories. The stunning views and beautiful landscapes are always worth the effort.

Gettin' there: The city of Fort Davis lies approximately 40 miles south of I-10. From the interstate, exit U.S. 290 to Balmorhea (if you have time, be sure to stop for a dip in the beautiful spring-fed pool at Balmorhea State Park). Turn south on Texas 17 and then west on Texas 118. Davis Mountains State Park and Indian Lodge are located four miles northwest of Fort Davis off Texas 118.

Black Bear Restaurant
Davis Mountains State Park
Box 786
Fort Davis, TX 79734
915/426-3254

Stop by and see: The Chihuahuan Desert Research Institute, located 4 miles south of Fort Davis on Texas 118, features a botanical garden containing more than 500 species of Chihuahuan plants. The institute also has a greenhouse filled with cacti for sale, a small gift shop, and a beautiful hiking trail.

Tortilla Soup
4 cups chicken, cooked and chopped
1½ cups chopped onion
8 ribs celery, chopped
2 jalapeño peppers, chopped
2 cloves garlic, minced
¼ cup vegetable oil
1 32-ounce can tomatoes

179

¼ cup chopped cilantro
1 teaspoon cumin
1 tablespoon chili powder
2 cups uncooked rice
½ can #10 (6½- or 7¼-pound) can corn
1 gallon chicken bouillon
12 corn tortillas

Place stock pot over medium heat and heat pot. Pour oil into pot and heat. Add onion, celery, jalapeños, and chicken. In another pot, boil bouillon and add to stock pot. Bring to a boil, and add rice, cumin, chili powder, and minced garlic. Add corn and canned tomatoes. Reduce heat and simmer for 50 minutes.

Meanwhile, cut tortillas into ½-inch strips and fry until crisp. Serve soup with tortilla strips.

Customers who order Mexican food at the Black Bear get a basket of chips and a small cup of this hot sauce. The recipe makes a bunch.

Chili Gringo

1 58-ounce can chopped green chili peppers
1 29-ounce can whole peeled tomatoes

Coarsely grind tomatoes in blender. Drain green chilies. Mix tomatoes and green chilies. Chill. Serve with chips.

Fort Stockton

Sarah's Cafe
(1929)

Local politicians, oil men, and ranchers at noon pack Sarah's Cafe, the oldest restaurant in Fort Stockton. Sarah Ramirez Nunez, one of 11 children raised in Shafter, Texas, opened the cafe in 1929. In the beginning, the restaurant, located in a small adobe building, could only serve 16 people at a time.

Through the years, Sarah and her family expanded the cafe, which now seats 80 customers. In 1965 Sarah's daughter and son-in-law, Cleo and Mike Castelo, bought the business. Their son, Michael David, now manages the cafe, still housed in the original adobe building on Nelson Street.

The long and extensive menu at Sarah's Cafe lists ONLY Mexican food. You won't find a chicken-fried steak smothered in cream gravy or even a hamburger here, though French fries are served with a few dinners. Not to worry, though. There's plenty from which to choose. In addition to the usual combination plates, Sarah's serves barbacoa, chile rellenos, burritos, tacos, fajitas, guacamole salad, and chalupas. Don Miguel's chicken-fried steak is served a la Mexicana with cheese, green sauce, rice, beans, and tortillas. Sarah's Delight, a chopped sirloin topped with chile salsa and cheese, comes with refried beans and Spanish rice.

In the late forties Sarah's served sandwiches and fountain specials in addition to enchiladas and tacos. Back then, 80 cents could buy a Mexican plate lunch. A burger and milk shake went for 20 cents each, and a malted milk for a quarter. Even the old 1960s prices sound good—T-bone, $2; Mexican plate lunch, $1.50; hamburger, 35 cents; and pie, 20 cents.

Though prices are higher, the food's just as good as it's ever been at Sarah's Cafe in Fort Stockton.

Gettin' there: From I-10, exit Highway 67/385 to Fort Stockton. The main thoroughfare is Dickinson Boulevard. Just west of the railroad tracks, turn south on Nelson Street.

Sarah's Cafe
106 S. Nelson St.
Fort Stockton, TX 79735
915/336-7700

Stop by and see: See the town's namesake, historic Fort Stockton established in 1867 (300 E. Third St.). Four of the original buildings still remain. For a historical overview of the area, the Annie Riggs Memorial Museum at 301 S. Main St.

features displays on archaeology, geology, pioneers, and ranching.

San Angelo

Zentner's Daughter Steak House
(1975)

As a little girl, Betty Zentner always aspired for one thing—to own a famous steak house just like her father's. In 1975 her dream came true when she opened Zentner's Daughter Steak House in San Angelo. The restaurant was an instant hit with local residents. That's because in the region, the family name Zentner is synonymous with great steaks, thanks to Betty's late father, John Zentner.

Born in 1899 in Falls County (southeast of Waco), Zentner and his family moved via horse-drawn wagons to Rowena, a tiny community northeast of San Angelo. His father first tried farming but abandoned the venture to open a grocery store and saloon. Some years later the elder Zentner established a meat business.

John Zentner's interest in cooking began during his teenage years when he flipped meat patties at a little burger joint. At age 18 he enlisted in the Army and worked two years as a cook at Fort Sam Houston in San Antonio. After his discharge he worked in Oregon as a butcher. Later he returned to West Texas, where he bought and transported cattle to Fort Worth. In 1946 he opened his first steak house, the original Lowake Inn, near Rowena. The next year he sold the business, bought it back two years later, then sold it again. In 1951 Zentner returned to the restaurant business when he opened the Lowake Steak House a mile away from Lowake Inn. He also opened and operated other restaurants in San Angelo, Rowena, Buffalo Gap, and Del Rio. The Lowake Inn has since closed, but the Lowake Steak House hasn't skipped a beat in all these years.

In his last years Zentner, who died in 1994 at the age of 94, supervised the kitchen and meat purchasing for his daughter's restaurant. To this day Betty and her staff prepare their grain-fed, aged beef the Zentner way—dusted with flour and garlic, then grilled to perfection. But steaks aren't the only item on the menu at Zentner's Daughter. There are also chicken-fried steak, several chicken selections, crab, shrimp, and catfish in addition to a number of appetizers, sandwiches, salads, and desserts.

Like her famous dad, Betty has established her own well-known reputation for great steaks and fine dining. Seems she comes by her abilities naturally. "I teethed on a T-bone because I was raised in a steak house all my life," she says simply. "I guess you could call me the beef baroness of West Texas. I've run more beef through these doors than most ranchers have run in their lifetime."

Gettin' there: Highway 87 South intersects with Knickerbocker Road inside the city. Turn west on Knickerbocker Road. Go about a mile until you see the San Angelo Stadium on the right. On the left will be the Stadium Park Shopping Center. There you'll find Zentner's Daughter.

Zentner's Daughter Steak House
1901 Knickerbocker Rd.
San Angelo, TX 76904
915/949-2821

Another family restaurant:
Zentner's Steak House
2715 Sherwood Way
San Angelo, TX 76901
915/942-8631

Stop by and see: Miss Hattie's Bordello Museum on Concho Avenue is the only one of its kind in Texas. Boards put up by the Texas Rangers, who raided the business in 1946, still cover all but the bordello's front windows.

Zentner's Daughter Chicken-Fried Steak
one tenderized portion of round steak

Coat steak in an egg-and-milk batter, then dip in a mixture
of flour, salt, pepper, and granulated garlic. Cook on top of
grill, not in grease.

▪▪▪▪▪▪▪▪▪▪▪▪▪▪▪▪▪▪▪▪▪▪▪▪

Sterling City

City Cafe
(1960s)

Everything's big in Texas, right? At least, that's what a lot of
folks assume. And when it comes to pancakes, it's definitely
true in Sterling City at the City Cafe, where Wesley Turner flips
the biggest ones in the state. No joke. These flapjacks are so big
they hang over the plate and make a mess on the table when
the syrup slides off the edges.

Wesley stumbled onto the jumbo idea one morning back in
1992 when he accidentally poured way too much pancake batter onto the grill. As the batter bubbled and browned, Wesley
decided he'd serve the hubcap-sized mistake anyway. Little did
he know that the pancake platter was headed for customers
who'd been having a bad day. By the time they'd finished what
they could of it, their demeanor had lightened considerably.
After a bit of musing, Wesley decided that adding Texas-sized
flapjacks to his menu might be a neat thing to do. So he did.
And today, a front window at the City Cafe proudly proclaims,
"Home of the Biggest Pancakes in Texas." For a buck fifty
apiece, the giant pancakes are an Epicurean bargain. Plus, one
easily feeds a family of three or four with leftovers to spare.

To make breakfast even more interesting, Wesley offers the
"Sterling City challenge." If a customer can down three, they're
free. Needless to say, Wesley sells very few stacks. Only two
brave souls have triumphed—amazingly, a 10-year-old boy and
a 90-year-old woman (took her nearly all day, though).

The City Cafe has been around since the 1960s. The build-ing was originally built in the thirties as a saloon. Later it housed a donut shop, followed by a pool hall, and finally a res-taurant. In the mid-eighties Wesley's mother bought the cafe, then Wesley bought it from her.

Besides pancakes for breakfast, the City Cafe also serves eggs (cooked your style), six kinds of omelettes, burritos, and French toast. For lunch and dinner, the menu offers steaks, "health meat choices" (grilled fish, chicken and pork chops), sandwiches, Mexican food (taco salads, tacos, enchiladas, and a traditional Mexican plate with rice and beans), a plentiful salad bar, and, of course, pie (chocolate meringue and coconut meringue). The food's plenty good here, but the flapjacks are THE talk of the table in Sterling City.

"I can guarantee two things about these pan-cakes," Wesley promises. "You're gonna get full. And you're gonna remember where you got 'em."

No joke.

Gettin' there: Sterling City is 43 miles northwest of San Angelo on U.S. 87.

City Cafe
622 Fourth St.
Sterling City, TX 76951
915/378-2029

Wesley's Recipe for the Biggest Batch of Pancakes in Texas

Take a number three wash tub and fill halfway with pancake batter mix. Add a heaping helping of generosity and an equal portion of gratitude. Add water and stir with large shovel until consistency of joint compound. Pour liberally on hot grill until diameter equals that of a 1957 Buick hubcap. Cook until batter bubbles with humor, then flip with shovel. Cook one minute, then serve with a smile on a large turkey platter. (Leftovers make great mattress pads, seat cushions, and saddle blankets as well as insulation for your home.)

Smothered Pork Chops

5 or 6 4-ounce pork chops
1 large can cream of chicken soup
1 small can cream of broccoli soup
½ cup chopped onions
2 cups flour
salt, pepper

Dredge pork chops in flour, salt, and pepper. Fry in an iron skillet until almost done. Place in a baking pan and add just enough water to cover. Add onion and soups, cover and bake at 350 degrees for two hours or until they are melt-in-your-mouth tender. Serve over white or brown rice, and top with parsley flakes.

Sweetwater

Allen's Family Style Meals
(1952)

Generations of the Allen family have worked and literally lived at Allen's Family Style Meals restaurant. Lizzie B. Allen, known affectionately as Ma Allen, opened the business in 1952 in her four-room frame home. She cooked meals and fed customers all they could eat for 75 cents.

"My father, Bill, was born here," says owner Billy Allen. "My grandmother knocked out a wall and used a wooden table that her sons built. Business got better so she knocked out another wall and then another wall. We still have the old table, and we serve off it every day. It's about 12 foot long."

Bill Allen worked in construction until 1968 when he joined his mother's business. He bought a panel truck and borrowed $500 to start a catering service. But he never had to use the money so he returned it.

Billy spent much of his own childhood in the kitchen with his grandmother. "I used to sit on the flour can while my family was working," he says. "I was too little to do anything so I'd watch while my grandmother made apple and cherry pies. Then I'd get to lick the pans." These days Billy, along with his sisters, Teresa Turnbow and Suzanne Nazworth, do all the cooking and baking for the restaurant.

As the restaurant's name implies, meals are served family style from 11 A.M. to 2 P.M. No menus here. Instead, Billy and his friendly staff set bowls and bowls of food on your table. When a bowl is nearly empty, another is brought in its place. "It's just like you're at home," he says. "We bring it out, and folks get after it. We usually have twelve different vegetables, three to four salads, and two meats. We have fried chicken every day, and then roast beef or barbecue sausage, meat loaf

187

or ham. The price also includes hot rolls, tea, and dessert, which is usually peach cobbler."

Never mind advertising. The Allens don't, except in the local school annuals. Still, people from as far away as New York and Chicago have heard about the restaurant and even gone more than a 100 miles out of their way to eat here.

News gets around whenever it involves good food.

Gettin' there: From I-20, take Business 20 (Broadway Street) and head for downtown. The restaurant is 1 mile east of the courthouse.

Allen's Family Style Meals
1301 E. Broadway St.
Sweetwater, TX 79556
915/235-2060

Other old-time restaurants:

Big Spring
Alberto's Crystal Cafe (1974)
120 E. Second St.
Big Spring, TX 79720
915/267-9024

Del Rio
Wright's Steak House (1978)
Highway 90 W
Del Rio, TX 78840
830/775-2621

El Paso
Elmer's Family Restaurant (1945)
6305 Montana Ave.
El Paso, TX 79925
915/778-5485

Marfa
Mike's Place (1952)
111 S. Highland Ave.
Marfa, TX 79843
915/729-8146

Rowena
Lowake Steak House (1951)
RR 1
Rowena, TX 76875
915/442-3201

San Angelo
Dun-Bar East Restaurant (1958)
1728 Pulliam
San Angelo, TX 76903
915/655-8780

Sonora
Sutton County Steakhouse (1974)
1306 N. Service Rd.
Sonora, TX 76950
915/387-3833

Uvalde
Amber Sky Coffee Shop (1960s)
2001 E. Main St.
Uvalde, TX 78801
830/278-3923

In the heart of Texas

Austin

Dairy Queen
(1947)

A red, ellipse-shaped Dairy Queen sign possesses an almost magical power, as any parent well knows. Pass one of those "Texas stop signs" on the highway, and you're sure to hear an instant reaction from the back seat. "Can we stop? Can we get some ice cream? Please? Please? PLEEEEAAAASSSSEEEE????"

I know. I'm one of those kids who's now getting paid back as a parent.

The first Dairy Queen opened in Joliet, Illinois, in June 1940. The company was a cooperative effort between J.F. McCullough, who owned the Homemade Ice Cream Co. in Green River, Illinois, and Harry Oltz, who'd invented a soft-serve ice cream dispenser. What should they name their new business? McCullough suggested Dairy Queen. After all, he reasoned, the cow is queen of the dairy industry.

The start of World War II in 1941 held back Dairy Queen's growth. Though customers loved the ice cream, war rationing made dairy products hard to come by. Ice cream, whenever it was available at one of the ten stores, would quickly sell out, and the store would close for the rest of the month. As soon as the war ended, though, Dairy Queen quickly expanded, and by 1947 the company had 100 outlets across the country.

One of them was the first Dairy Queen in Texas, a white, crackerbox stand opened by O.W. Klose in Austin at 29th and Guadalupe Streets. Klose was a 63-year-old grocer from Illinois who'd frequented a local Dairy Queen with his granddaughter. He wondered if he could get a machine like that and ended up with the rights to sell Dairy Queen ice cream in Texas. Armed with his own soft-serve dispenser, he moved to Texas. His 36-year-old son, Rolly, later joined him, and the two franchised

Dairy Queens across the state. Rolly later bought out his father, who died in 1950. In 1980 Rolly Klose sold his Dairy Queen rights back to the company's home office in Minneapolis.

In its heyday, 1,008 Dairy Queens in 1980 operated across Texas. Today 722 stores, all independently owned, dot the state. Worldwide the count stands at more than 5,800.

Until the 1950s Dairy Queens touted only its frozen treat in sundaes, cones, and take-home pints and quarts. Then an owner in Georgia started experimenting with a hot-food menu, and the Brazier food line of burgers, fries, and more was born. In Texas and some adjacent states, Dairy Queens cook up a "Texas" line of burgers that includes the Dude, HungerBuster, and Beltbuster.

Admittedly, DQ burgers do taste good, but we grown-up kids all know from where the magical power of a Texas stop sign comes. . . .

"OK, OK! WE'LL STOP AND GET YOU SOME ICE CREAM!! NOW PLEASE BE QUIET AND LET ME DRIVE!!!"

Green Pastures Restaurant
(1946)

One of the most elegant and best loved restaurants in Austin is Green Pastures, housed in an old two-story Victorian home south of downtown. Tucked behind a white picket fence and surrounded by towering live oak trees, the restaurant has hosted generations of memorable meals and special celebrations.

Dr. E.W. Herndon, a physician, lawyer, and minister, built the mansion in 1894 and raised poultry on part of the property. In 1916 attorney Henry Faulk and his wife, Martha, bought the land and moved into the white frame house with their five children.

In later years daughter Mary Faulk married Chester Koock, and the couple lived in the big old house. For fun, she coordinated children's parties. "I really don't know how it did all come about, but I decided to make this a paying hobby," she wrote in *The Texas Cookbook*, her collection of Texas recipes and anecdotes published in 1965. "Heaven knows we could use a little subsidy for the increasing number of little feet pattering around." (The Koocks had seven children of their own.) The party business soon evolved into a catering company. In 1946, at the insistence of friends and customers, Mary and Chester began serving lunch and dinner downstairs in the house, which had been bequeathed to them. She named the new venture "Green Pastures," in honor of her father's love of the place. In 1969 the Koocks retired and sold the restaurant to their son, Ken Koock, and his partner, Lee Buslett.

Today Mary's warm graciousness lingers in Green Pastures' richly decorated dining rooms and beautifully set tables. By candlelight, guests sip wine and share quiet conversation while dining on the finest of cuisine (always artfully prepared), such as grilled salmon (topped with an apple mint relish and served with sauteed spinach and rice), smoked boneless duck breast (stuffed with a mild serrano pepper, wrapped in bacon, and served with a black currant sauce), and asparagus strudel (asparagus, feta cheese, and sliced almonds in a phyllo pastry). Ah, and the desserts. . . . Chocolate Love (a rich chocolate cake layered with chocolate mousse), New Orleans-style bread pudding (a spicy, nutty delicacy served with a Jack Daniels sauce), a Texas Pecan Ball (a generous scoop of vanilla ice cream rolled in crushed pecans and topped with homemade fudge sauce), and bananas foster for two (a magnificent flambe of bananas, rum, orange, and brown sugar served over ice cream).

A Texas Historical Marker medallion on the front porch honors Green Pastures' century-old heritage, which is sure to continue for decades more.

Gettin' there: From I-35, take the Oltorf Street exit and turn west onto Oltorf. At Congress Avenue, turn north. Turn west on Live Oak Street.

Green Pastures Restaurant
811 W. Live Oak St.
Austin, TX 78704
512/444-1888

Stop by and see: Did you know that the state capitol, completed in 1888, conceals thousands of iron cannon balls within its granite walls? During renovation of the capitol in 1994, workers cut into walls to install central heat and air and discovered the balls. Closer examination of the granite blocks revealed the innovative construction method used by Scottish stone makers who worked on the seven-year project. On the top and bottom surfaces of a granite block, the artisans cut two parallel grooves (which formed a square) with half-moon indentions at each corner. As the granite blocks were rolled into place atop the cannon balls, the balls fell into the depressions, and the blocks locked into place.

Mary Koock served this delicious favorite to her guests at Green Pastures. Customers still enjoy her "milk punch" tradition every Sunday during the restaurant's luncheon buffet.

Milk Punch
3 cups vanilla ice cream
1½ cups milk
½ cup bourbon
¼ cup white rum
1 jigger brandy
3 ice cubes
nutmeg

Combine ice cream, milk, bourbon, rum, brandy, and ice cubes in blender. Blend until ice cream is liquefied and mixture has smooth texture of a thin milk shake. Serve in wine glasses and sprinkle with nutmeg. Makes about 5 cups.

Green Pastures' Duck Texanna
Seed four serrano peppers. Cut into strips. Lay two duck breasts on a clean surface. Lay peppers lengthwise in center of meat. Roll breasts and wrap with 2 to 4 pieces of uncooked bacon. Secure with toothpicks. Grill long enough to cook bacon (smoke for 45 minutes at 250 degrees). Slice into roulades and serve with Black Currant Sauce. Serves 2.

Green Pastures' Black Currant Sauce
Mix together in a pot and set aside:
6 ounces black currant jelly
1 cup beef stock
1 cup chicken stock

In a separate pan, stir together over low heat until sugar is dissolved:
1½ tablespoons brown sugar
½ cup raspberry vinegar

Add sugar mixture to stock. Thicken with cornstarch, water, salt, and pepper. Simmer for 30 to 40 minutes. Fold in 2 tablespoons black currants and serve.

Texas Historical Marker Green Pastures

This Victorian home, located on the 1835 Isaac Decker Grant, was built in 1894-95 by Dr. E. W. Herndon and sold in 1912 to Judge W. W. Burnett. It became the residence in 1916 of lawyer Henry Faulk (1867-1939), his wife, Martha (Miner), (1878-1957), and their children, Hamilton, Martha, Mary, John Henry, and Texana. Naming the home "Green Pastures," Mary and her husband, Chester Koock, opened it for public dining in 1946. It was purchased in 1969 by their son Ken Koock and Lee Buslett.

Hut's Hamburgers
(1939)

Homer "Hut" Hutson opened the first Hut's Hamburgers in 1939 on South Congress Avenue. He moved the burger joint in 1959 and then to its present location on West Sixth Street in 1969. In 1981 Shoal Creek flooded and devastated nearby buildings. Miraculously, Hut's Hamburgers sustained little damage. Today, folks line up to eat at the little fifties-style cafe that sits perilously close to the street curb. Inside, the walls are plastered with framed photos, newspaper clippings, and other mementos. You can sit at the counter on a stool or claim a table or booth.

Most customers order burgers here. And these aren't ordinary burgers. At Hut's, you can choose from 20 varieties of the all-American sandwich. The choices include Mel's Number 2 (mustard, pickles and onions), Beachboy's Favorite (pineapple, Swiss cheese, mayo, lettuce, and bell peppers), Mr. Blue (bleu cheese dressing, Swiss cheese, bacon, and lettuce), and Tuby's Tickler (chili, jalapeños, and grated cheese). If ground beef's not your thing, you can order a buffalo patty, chicken breast, or veggie patty instead. Talk about decisions!

At Hut's, blue plate specials vary by the day. Monday features fried chicken; Tuesday, chicken-fried steak; Wednesday, ham steak; Thursday, meat loaf; and Friday, fried catfish (all served with French fries or mashed potatoes, vegetable, Texas toast, and coffee or tea). But don't worry—you can still order chicken-fried steak as a plate dinner any day of the week. Need more choices? How about a dozen different sandwiches, several salads, peppered onion rings, buffalo wings, home-made soup, and nachos.

No burger joint is complete unless it serves thick and creamy malts and shakes. Hut's is no exception. You can also indulge in a Frozen Jolt-a-Matic (brewed espresso in a shake) or a slice of Mud Pie (chocolate and coffee ice cream on a chocolate wafer crust and topped with hot fudge).

I vote for Tuby's Tickler and the Jolt. Both are worth standing in line for.

Gettin' there: From I-35, exit Sixth Street and go west. Cross Congress Avenue. Hut's is on the south side of West Sixth Street, just past Nueces Street.

Hut's Hamburgers
807 W. Sixth St.
Austin, TX 78703
512/472-0693

Stop by and see: The Zilker Botanical Garden at 2220 Barton Springs Rd. has gardens galore. You can explore collections of herbs, roses, azaleas, cacti and succulents, and butterfly-attracting plants. You'll also see an Oriental garden and a xeriscape demonstration garden.

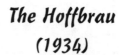

The Hoffbrau
(1934)

Depending on the temperature outside, it's best to dress accordingly when you eat at The Hoffbrau, a little hole-in-the-wall steak house on West Sixth Street.

"This building has no air conditioning or heat," explains owner Mary Gail Hamby Ray. "So if it's 30 degrees outside, it's about 50 in here. If it's 100 outside, it's 80 inside."

As you can surmise, dining at The Hoffbrau (German for "beer garden") is a no-frills epicurean experience. Little has changed since Mary Gail's grandfather, Coleman Hamby, and his brother, Thomas, started the short-order restaurant during the Depression in 1934. Pull up a metal folding chair to one of the rickety tables, and Mary Gail will gladly share her family's story.

"My grandfather had lost several jobs and was an ice man before he bought this property for $250," she says. "It had been a feed store, and it'd been vacant for a while. The owner needed money for her sick husband. They owned the Fischer Brothers Grocery Store."

"My grandfather and great uncle opened The Hoffbrau about the same time the Prohibition laws were repealed. At first they didn't sell much food. People mostly bought draft beer. In the forties, a lot of soldiers were stationed at Bergstrom Air Force Base. They'd come in with big appetites for beef and big money to spend. So my grandfather purchased a little grill. His steaks caught on, and we've been selling them ever since."

During the forties, Coleman's sons, Robert and Thomas Hamby, got out of high school and joined the business. Gradually they took over more and more responsibilities. After the deaths of their uncle and father, the brothers ran the Hoffbrau. "They lived next door to one another," Mary Gail says. "They were very close. Sometimes they'd have an argument, get mad at each other, and close up for the day. They died on the same day two years apart."

Mary Gail Ray (Robert's daughter) and her husband, Ruben, have run The Hoffbrau since 1991. They've kept everything the same, including the old wooden tables (since covered with peachy orange Formica), originally built at a cost of $1.10 each. "When we change anything, people don't like it very much," Mary Gail explains. "People like to come back to a place that hasn't changed very much."

They've kept the menu the same, too—sparse and simple. "We sell small and large T-bones, and small and large sirloins," Mary Gail says. "We've never had a printed menu." Steaks are cooked to perfection on a grill in a corner of the dining room, then plopped on a platter and brushed with a lemon-butter sauce that mixes with the steak's juices. Customers also get a Hoffbrau salad (lettuce, tomatoes, and bits of green olives soaked in the house dressing, a blend of fresh garlic, lemon, and oil), sliced Butter-Krust bread, crackers, and chunky steak fries. "We peel a lot of pounds of potatoes every day, sometimes 400 pounds on a Friday," Mary Gail adds.

Other Hoffbraus have sprung up around the state (like in Dallas, Beaumont, Houston, New Braunfels, and San Antonio), but The Hoffbrau in Austin stands as the original. And no matter how hard you try, you won't find anything fancy about it. But if it's extra busy, you might find yourself sharing a table with a stranger, someone famous or otherwise. "We've had legislators and governors eat here," Mary Gail says with a grin. "Bikers, too. We get people from all walks of life."

Gettin' there: From I-35, exit Sixth Street and go west. Cross Congress Avenue. The Hoffbrau is on the south side of West Sixth Street, just past Nueces Street.

The Hoffbrau
613 W. Sixth St.
Austin, TX 78701
512/472-0822

Stop by and see: The remains of nine governors, more than 2,000 Civil War soldiers, and a number of other colorful Texas residents are buried in the Texas State Cemetery at East Seventh and Comal Streets. Wander in between the graves, and you'll find the tombstones of Stephen F. Austin (the "Father of Texas"), naturalist Gideon Lincecum, and folklorist J. Frank Dobie (a relative of mine—he was a first cousin to my grandfather, Dudley R. Dobie). Sculptures by Elisabet Ney and Pompeo Coppini mark several graves.

Some Texas trivia: The state's shortest highway, State Road Spur 165 (eight-tenths of a mile long), loops through the cemetery.

Matt's El Rancho
(1952)

Hungry for chips and salsa, enchiladas and beans? Matt's El Rancho has been dishing them up for decades. This Austin institution was started by Matt Martinez, one of six children born to Delfino and Maria Martinez of Austin. At an early age, Matt learned the restaurant business from his father, who owned the first Mexican food restaurant on Congress Avenue. In 1944 Matt married his wife, Janie, and the couple in 1952 opened Matt's El Rancho on East First Street. At first they served only blue plate specials, like chicken-fried steak. But when the occasional enchilada special drew so many raves, the Martinezes decided to expand and serve more Tex-Mex dishes. Soon Janie's Mexican specialties dominated the menu. Meanwhile, Matt worked hard at building the restaurant's clientele. He passed out business cards, matchbooks, and El Rancho postcards. Word spread, and customers increased. Eventually, the couple opened El Rancho #2 not far from their original restaurant.

After 34 years the two restaurants outgrew their buildings in East Austin. So Matt and Janie bought a tree-shaded lot on South Lamar and in 1986 built a huge new building with three dining rooms, a patio, a large bar, and a tortilleria.

Through the years the Martinzes and their four children have pioneered several popular foods. Matt Jr. conjured up the "Bob Armstrong Dip," an appetizer on the restaurant's menu. Named for the long-time Texas Land Commissioner (who frequented the restaurant), the layered dip consists of chile con queso, guacamole, and taco meat. The restaurant also serves a repertoire of rich salsas, and a different one is made fresh every day.

Besides enchiladas, Matt's serves an abundance of other tempting dishes—fajitas (beef, chicken, shrimp, and vegetarian), Mexican-style seafood, tamales, chicken mole, tacos, grilled steaks, burritos, Mexican pizza, and—oh, yes—chicken-fried steaks. For dessert, there's puffy sopapillas, flan, and pralines.

Gettin' there: From I-35, exit at Oltorf Street and turn west. At Lamar Boulevard, turn south. Matt's is on the left-hand side of the street.

Matt's El Rancho
2613 S. Lamar Blvd.
Austin, TX 78704
512/462-9333

Stop by and see: At the National Wildflower Research Center (4801 La Crosse Ave.) in Southwest Austin, wildflowers aren't the only stars. Founded in 1982 by Lady Bird Johnson, the wildflower center is the only national nonprofit organization dedicated to the study, preservation, and reestablishment of native wildflowers, grasses, shrubs, and trees in planned landscapes.

These recipes are from Matt Martinez Jr.'s cookbook, *Matt Martinez's Culinary Frontier: A Real Texas Cookbook*.

Chile con Queso
1 tablespoon oil of your choice
½ cup finely chopped sweet white onion
½ cup finely chopped bell pepper or jalapeño (or a combination)
1 teaspoon ground cumin
1 teaspoon granulated garlic
½ teaspoon salt
2 tablespoons cornstarch
1 cup water or canned chicken broth
8 ounces shredded cheese (Kraft American is best)
1 cup chopped tomatoes

Using a thick, heavy pot, heat the oil and saute the onion and the dry ingredients for 2 to 3 minutes, until the onion is translucent. Add the water or broth, and heat 3 to 4 minutes, allowing the sauce to thicken, then add the shredded cheese and tomatoes. Carefully simmer the queso on low heat for 3 to 5 minutes, adjusting its thickness to suit your taste by adding water or cheese. Serve hot. Makes 6 to 8 servings.

Migas
¼ cup oil of your choice
12 corn tortillas
½ cup coarsely chopped onion
6 eggs

1 cup coarsely chopped tomatoes
1 large jalapeño or 3 serrano chile peppers, finely chopped
½ teaspoon black pepper
¾ teaspoon salt
1 teaspoon crushed and finely chopped garlic
1 cup shredded Monterey jack or American cheese

In a large skillet, heat the oil to 350 degrees. Cut or tear the tortillas into bite-size pieces. Saute the tortillas until they are crisp. Add the onion and saute for about 1 minute. In a bowl, beat the eggs. Add the tomatoes, chile peppers, black pepper, salt, and garlic, and thoroughly beat them into the eggs. Pour the egg mixture onto the tortillas. Cook the eggs 3 or 4 minutes, until they begin to set, stirring and flipping them in the process. Add the cheese and continue stirring and flipping until the eggs are completely set. Migas are best served immediately with refried beans, flour tortillas, and your favorite hot sauce. Makes 4 to 6 servings.

Optional: For spicier, meatier migas, add 1 cup of your favorite sausage, bacon, chorizo, or chopped ham at the time the onions are added.

Chile Rellenos
Ranchero Salsa:
2 tablespoons vegetable oil
1 cup finely chopped white onions
½ cup finely chopped celery
½ cup finely chopped bell pepper
1 teaspoon ground cumin
½ teaspoon dried oregano
1 teaspoon granulated garlic
¼ teaspoon black pepper
1 tablespoon cornstarch
1½ teaspoons salt
1 14-ounce can whole tomatoes (cut up)
2 cups chicken or beef broth

To prepare the salsa, use a heavy sauce pot to heat the oil and brown the onions, celery, and bell pepper for 2 to 3 minutes. Add the remaining ingredients and simmer for 20 minutes on low heat. Use while the sauce is still warm, or refrigerate for later.

For the meat:
1 pound ground beef

1 teaspoon salt
2 teaspoons ground cumin
1½ teaspoon granulated garlic
½ teaspoon black pepper
¼ cup finely chopped sweet white onion
3 tablespoons finely chopped celery
3 tablespoons finely chopped bell pepper

To prepare the meat, combine the meat ingredients in a 10-inch skillet. Saute the meat over a medium heat for 4 to 5 minutes, until thoroughly cooked.

For the rest:
oil for frying
6 fresh Anaheim peppers
2 cups flour
½ teaspoon salt
¼ teaspoon black pepper
2 cups buttermilk
2 cups grated American cheese
¼ cup raisins
¼ cup chopped pecans

Preheat oven to 350 degrees. Completely wipe down and dry the Anaheim peppers. In a skillet, heat oil to a depth of ¾ to 1 inch. Roll the whole peppers around in the hot oil for 60 to 90 seconds, causing them to blister. Remove the peppers, wrap them in a damp cloth, and let them sit for 5 to 10 minutes. Then remove the pepper skins, split each pepper, seed and remove all the membranes.

In a bowl, mix the flour, salt, and black pepper. Dust the peppers in the flour mixture, roll them in buttermilk, and dust each again in the flour. Fry the peppers in the oil over moderate heat until the batter is golden.

Arrange the fried peppers in an ovenproof dish. Divide the meat evenly over the tops of the peppers, then sprinkle with cheese. Bake for 4 to 5 minutes, until the cheese starts to melt. While the dish is still in the oven, add the raisins and pecans, and continue baking for 1 or 2 minutes, until the cheese starts to bubble. Serve immediately with Matt's Ranchera Salsa. Makes 3-4 servings.

Bandera

O.S.T. Restaurant
(1921)

Ask what "O.S.T." stands for, and you'll get a mini lesson in Texas history. According to the restaurant's menu, the acronym stands for "Old Spanish Trail, a famous route started by missionaries and used by Spanish explorers and settlers that ran through Bandera." The network of trails in Texas had other names, too—the Old San Antonio Road, Camino Real, the King's Highway, and the San Antonio-Nacogdoches Road.

In Bandera the O.S.T. Restaurant opened in 1921. The building originally housed an old grocery store, and where the restaurant's John Wayne room now stands was once a horse corral. During the thirties and forties, the O.S.T. was also a dance hall where lots of well-known singers and bands performed.

Because Bandera touts itself as the "Cowboy Capital of the World," the O.S.T. features lots of Western touches, like wagon wheel chandeliers, a trophy elk, a display of spurs, and a "saddle" bar, where customers can help themselves to a daily buffet. The aforementioned John Wayne room features dozens of photos of the Duke and other cowboys and celebrities.

As for good food, the O.S.T.'s got plenty. For breakfast, the menu offers eggs, omelettes, migas, egg enchiladas (scrambled eggs and cheddar cheese rolled in a corn tortilla and topped with green onions, ranchero sauce, and more cheese), pancakes, waffles, and cinnamon rolls. Among the menu's breakfast specials is a "wrangler's breakfast" plate, which comes with a grilled pork chop, two eggs, hash browns or grits, refried beans, and toast or biscuits.

For lunch and supper, the O.S.T., for a small-town cafe, serves up a surprising variety of food. Chicken-fried steak, of course, tops the list of steaks followed by a porterhouse T-bone, rib eye, hamburger steak, and a "Trail Boss Special," a breaded, deep-fried rib eye. Customers can also choose fried shrimp, catfish, grilled chicken, chicken strips, sandwiches, burgers, or a Mexican salad. Tex-Mex selections include enchiladas, tacos, chili rellenos, burritos, fajitas, chili, and chalupas.

And when all else on the menu fails to please . . . there at the bottom of the page is one magic word—"pizza."

Gettin' there: The O.S.T. is located on Main Street in downtown Bandera.

O.S.T. Restaurant
305 Main St.
Bandera, TX 78003
830/796-3836

Stop by and see: The Frontier Times Museum at 506 13th St. contains a variety of Old West relics, Western art, and Indian items.

"This cake tastes better a day or two later," advises Gwen Park, owner of the O.S.T. Restaurant.

Fudge Cake
2 cups flour
2 cups sugar
2 sticks margarine
4 tablespoons cocoa
1 cup water
½ cup buttermilk
2 eggs, beaten
1 teaspoon baking soda
1 teaspoon vanilla

Mix flour and sugar together in large mixing bowl. In saucepan, put margarine, cocoa, and water. Cook on medium heat until mixture boils. Add this to dry ingredients. In separate container, mix buttermilk and soda together; let sit for a minute. When it has risen a little, add it along with the beaten eggs and vanilla to cake mixture. Pour into a 13x9-inch pan sprayed with Pam. Bake at 400 degrees for about 20 minutes. Press the center. If it springs back, it's done. Top with icing while still hot.

Icing:
1 stick margarine
4 tablespoons cocoa
6 tablespoons milk
1 box powdered sugar
1 teaspoon vanilla
1 cup chopped pecans

Melt margarine with cocoa and milk. When dissolved, add sugar, vanilla, and pecans. Pour on hot cake.

▰▰▰▰▰▰▰▰▰▰▰▰▰▰▰▰▰▰▰▰

Blanco

Blanco Bowling Club and Cafe
(1947)

The sign hanging from the restaurant on Fourth Street reads "Blanco Bowling Club and Cafe." But folks around town—me included—simply call it the "Bowling Alley." The local coffee shop is as much a landmark in town as the majestic old courthouse on the square and the city cemetery down the road.

Roland and Viola Bindseil originally built the restaurant and bowling alley in 1947. After a string of managers, C. A. and Florence Weeaks bought the business in 1965. Two years later a group of Blanco folks joined hands, purchased the bowling alley, and turned it into a club. Today approximately 300 members pay dues of $5 a year. On weeknights the locals gather for German-style nine-pin bowling in the bowling hall, which adjoins the restaurant and serves as an additional dining room during the day. Twenty-two teams from the surrounding area compete for honors and trophies, some of which are proudly displayed in an aging glass case.

Like clockwork every morning, a group of dedicated domino players gather in the "bowling alley" hall to "rattle the bones" and drink coffee. About 20 men, mostly retired, drift in and out during the day to play. Plunk down in a chair, and you'll likely overhear some serious conversations along this vein:

"You don't have to help me, you rascal," growls one player. "I don't need them nickels." (In dominoes, the word "nickel" stands for five points.)

"All right, give us a nickel," chortles another. "I think I'm gonna domino."

"Aw, I don't think ya are," his opponent protests.

A player nursing a cigarette slings down a white piece, and the game concludes. The two losing partners must pay the price—one quarter each, money that is deposited in a faded cigar box.

"That's the rent we charge them," the man behind the bar explains. "The losers pay 50 cents, and they try hard to win. They hate to part with those quarters."

While the domino games unfold, stools at the counter and tables in the front dining room fill up for breakfast. At the "Big Table," as it's called (a long rectangular table near the counter), the regulars claim a chair while Tammy and Cindy, the personable waitresses, fill ceramic brown mugs with steaming coffee. As soon as someone finishes and leaves, someone else walks in the door and claims the vacant seat. Local ranchers, businessmen (like Butch Crofts, our local mortician), and cowboys talk about the weather, who's died recently, stock prices (and I don't mean Wall Street), street gossip, and the latest political shenanigans, both local and otherwise. Now and then someone feeling especially generous that morning picks up the coffee tab for the entire table, and everyone nods their appreciation.

For breakfast, the Bowling Alley serves fresh glazed donuts, cinnamon rolls, and cinnamon twists, all sugary sweet and rich. Folks also order biscuits, breakfast tacos, and eggs with hash browns. I like to order a BLT taco, an invention of my dear

211

friend the late Cyril Nevelow, who frequented the Big Table. In fact, thanks to him, I had a seat next to him at the Big Table whenever we met for breakfast there.

Lunch at the Bowling Alley always features a daily special. For example, a few bucks will buy you a plate of chicken strips, mashed potatoes with gravy, corn, a salad, and chocolate pudding along with generous slices of homemade bread. Mexican food and chicken-fried steaks also top the list of customer favorites. And oh, my, the cream pies ... they're baked fresh every morning with delicately browned meringues that reach a half mile high.

Pie and coffee at a bowling alley? Only in Blanco, folks.

Gettin' there: From Main Street/U.S. 281 (one and the same), turn east on Fourth Street. The Bowling Club is a block and a half down the street on the left.

Blanco Bowling Club and Cafe
310 Fourth St.
Blanco, TX 78606
830/833-4416

Stop by and see: Blanco State Park along the Blanco River (one of my favorite places in the world) is a great place to picnic and enjoy a refreshing dip in the water. By the way, my first and favorite husband, Terry, manages this little getaway. Stop by and say hi.

And because this is MY book, I can brag about our old limestone courthouse on the square. It was designed by architect F.E. Ruffini and completed in 1886. Four years later, though, Blanco lost its standing as county seat, and a new courthouse was built in Johnson City. After serving a variety of roles, the courthouse was privately purchased in 1986 and nearly dismantled. However, citizens banded together and formed the Old Blanco County Courthouse Preservation Society. After raising lots of money, the group in 1990 purchased the building and later restored the grand dame of downtown Blanco. Today the old courthouse serves as a community hall for weddings, meetings, dances, and other local events.

King Ranch Chicken Casserole

3 pounds chicken breasts or 1 whole cooked
chicken (reserve 1 cup broth)
1 large onion, chopped
1 large green pepper, chopped
2 tablespoons margarine
1 teaspoon chili powder
dash of garlic salt
1 can cream of chicken soup
1 can cream of mushroom soup
1 can Rotel tomatoes and green chilies, drained
and crushed
½ pound cheddar cheese, grated
12 corn tortillas, cut into strips

Bone and cut chicken into bite-size pieces. Saute onion and green peppers in margarine. Combine chili powder, garlic salt, soups, broth, and Rotel. Place half the chicken in a large casserole dish; top with half of soup mixture, tortilla strips, onion, green pepper, then cheese. Repeat layers. Bake, covered, at 350 degrees for 30 minutes. Bake, uncovered, for 15 minutes more. Serves 8.

Beef Stroganoff

$\frac{1}{2}$ cup minced onions
$\frac{1}{4}$ teaspoon garlic powder
$\frac{1}{4}$ cup butter
I pound ground beef
2 tablespoons flour
I teaspoon salt
I 8-ounce can mushrooms, sliced and drained
I can cream of chicken soup, undiluted
I cup sour cream

Saute onions and garlic in butter over medium heat; add beef and brown. Stir in flour, salt, pepper, and mushrooms. Cook 5 minutes. Stir in soup; simmer, uncovered, for 10 minutes. Stir in sour cream; heat through. Serve over egg noodles. Makes 4 to 6 servings.

Brady

Club Cafe

(1930s)

The Club Cafe in Brady has been around so long that folks can't remember when it opened. "We have people in their seventies and eighties who remember their parents bringing them here as kids," offers manager John Craig, the nephew of owner Ellaig Craig.

No matter. Folks still keep coming after all these years. As a result, everyone knows everyone by name at the Club Cafe. If you're just passing through and stopping by for lunch, you'll likely get some pleasant nods and smiles from the regulars.

Breakfast runs 'til 11 A.M. "Country breakfasts" range from a chicken-fried steak served with two eggs to three biscuits smothered in cream gravy. Tex-Mex selections include huevos rancheros (eggs topped with ranchero sauce), chorizo con huevos (Mexican sausage scrambled with two eggs), and breakfast tacos. The glazed donuts are "handmade by Maclovia Ramirez," boasts the menu.

Yes, you'll find the Texas favorite—chicken-fried steak—on the regular menu. It's there among the other beef and pork items, such as sirloin, rib eye, T-bone, liver and onions, steak fingers, pork chops, and ham steak. The Club Cafe has plenty of other good things, too, like appetizers (nachos, potato skins, and onion rings, to name a few), burgers, fried and grilled chicken, catfish, frog legs, Mexican plates, soups, salads, and sandwiches.

By the way, one of Brady's claims to fame is its geographical location—the city sits right "smack dab in the middle" of the state. As a special tribute, a stone Texas-shaped monument bearing a big red heart and the words "Heart of Texas—Brady"—stands in front of the 1900 McCulloch County courthouse.

Gettin' there: From U.S. 190 or U.S. 87, go west on 87 (West Commerce Street).

Club Cafe
506 W. Commerce St.
Brady, TX 76825
915/597-7522

Stop by and see: The true geographic center of Texas lies 5 miles northwest of a historical marker that stands on U.S. 377 (15 miles north of Brady). In straight-line distance, the center is 437 miles from the Rio Grande River at El Paso, 412 miles from the Panhandle border beyond Texline, 401 miles from the Rio Grande below Brownsville, and 341 miles from the Sabine River near Burkeville.

Chicken Soups

Chop one large onion and one stalk celery. Place in a large pot. Add salt, pepper, and one half of a chicken. Cover with water, and boil until chicken is done. Remove chicken, debone, chop, and return to broth.

For rice soup, add rice. For noodle soup, add noodles. For cream of chicken soup, thicken with cornstarch or flour. Add sweet red peppers (chopped), if you like.

Brownwood

Underwood's Cafeteria
(1951)

Some folks drive out of their way to eat at Underwood's Cafeteria. They go to relish the restaurant's juicy barbecue beef and crispy fried chicken, not to mention the delectable homemade rolls and hot fruit cobblers. Underwood's reputation is so widespread that it earned a ranking TWICE in *Texas Highways* magazine's "Texas's Top 10 Restaurants." The two readers' polls were conducted in 1992 and 1998.

Underwood's Cafeteria traces its beginnings back to a small building on West Commerce, where M.E. Underwood first sold barbecue in 1951. His sons later expanded the successful business and opened cafeterias in San Angelo, Lubbock, Abilene, Wichita Falls, Fort Worth, Dallas, Arlington, Waxahachie, and even Oklahoma. Today only the Brownwood location (run by M.E.'s son, Leonard) and a second cafeteria in Waco are left.

For to-go eating or sit-down dining, Underwood's dishes up generous portions of barbecue beef, German sausage, ribs, and

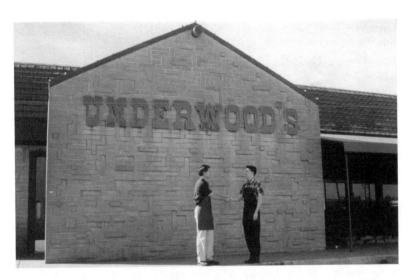

chicken, served with all the trimmings. Mama Underwood's fried chicken comes with mashed potatoes and cream gravy. The cafeteria also serves chicken-fried steak and fried catfish. Believe it or not, folks also rave about the restaurant's vegetables—red beans, carrots, green beans, corn, mashed potatoes, coleslaw, and potato salad. And the peach, apple, and cherry cobblers? Some folks eat a bowl, then order more to take home.

By the way, when you visit Underwood's in Brownwood, you'll see Elmo, the 20-foot-tall cowboy who towers over the restaurant. The "billboard" cowboy, clad in a white apron, hat, boots, and a kerchief tie, holds a dinner bell and beckons passersby to stop in. Morris Underwood, Leonard's brother, designed the cowboy sign, and his nephew (Leonard's son), Paul Underwood, christened it "Elmo," the middle name of many generations of Underwood men.

Gettin' there: Underwood's is located at the intersection of U.S. 67 and 84.

Underwood's Cafeteria
404 W. Commerce
Brownwood, TX 76801
915/646-6110

Comfort

Cypress Creek Inn
(1952)

Cypress Creek Inn is the oldest restaurant in Comfort, a quiet little town on the banks of the Guadalupe River in the Hill Country. Damon and Charlotte Holmes in 1952 opened the original restaurant, which perched above Cypress Creek on Highway 27. After Damon died in the early eighties, Charlotte ran the business with help from her family.

In 1981 a 14-year-old boy by the name of Sergio Rodriguez started working part time at the restaurant. He stayed on the payroll through high school and on weekends and summers through his college years. After college he returned to the Inn. This time he cooked, waited tables, AND managed the business. Then he took a huge step.

"In 1995 I had the opportunity to purchase the business," Sergio says. And he did. Customers never batted an eye. "I'd been cooking at the restaurant for 15 years so the food quality never changed when I took over. Some of the same employees stayed with me, and some are still here to this day."

When Sergio had to move the restaurant in 1996 to a new location, his faithful employees and customers went, too. "After 43 years of being in the same location, the building went up for sale, so I had to relocate the Inn," he explains. As a result, Cypress Creek moved one and a half blocks closer to town into an existing building.

Thanks to Sergio's dedication to keeping the restaurant going, folks can still count on the Inn's daily specials, such as baked pork chops on Wednesdays, grilled chicken breasts on Thursdays, baked meat loaf on Fridays, and Swiss steak on Saturdays. Sundays feature roast beef, baked ham, baked barbecue chicken, and steaks. Turkey and dressing is served the first Sunday of each month. All specials include a salad, tea or coffee, two (three on Sundays) veggie sides, and a slice of pie. "Not many places include dessert with their meals anymore," Sergio says.

"We're not a fancy place," he adds. "Just a place to come and get great food at a reasonable price."

Gettin' there: From I-10, exit Comfort and head west on Texas 27. Cypress Creek Inn is located at 408 Highway 27.

Cypress Creek Inn
408 Highway 27
Comfort, TX 78013
830/995-3977

Stop by and see: The Ingenhuett Store on High Street stands as a living tribute to a vanishing segment of American social history—the general store.

Coconut-Buttermilk Pie

1 ½ cups buttermilk
1 cup sugar
1 cup coconut
3 eggs
3 tablespoons flour
1 teaspoon vanilla
¼ teaspoon nutmeg
1 stick margarine
1 9-inch deep-dish pie shell

Melt margarine; mix in sugar and flour. Add eggs, vanilla, and nutmeg. Mix well. Add nutmeg and buttermilk. Mix again. Stir in coconut and pour into pie shell. Bake for 55 minutes at 325 degrees.

Corn Pudding Casserole

2 cans cream-style corn
2 eggs
crumbs of one hamburger bun
2 slices cheese
1 ¼ cups milk
dab of margarine
salt and sugar to taste

Combine all ingredients and pour into greased 8x8-inch pan.
Bake for one hour at 325 degrees or until firm.

Fredericksburg

Andy's Diner
(1957)

Bulls by the dozen get shot on a regular basis in Andy's Diner.

But only figuratively speaking. The bull shootin' gets done every morning here around a table affectionately known as the Bull Table. That's where local ranchers and farmers have gathered for more than 40 years to drink coffee and discuss the daily news.

"We have three groups that come," says owner Don Wise. "The first group arrives at 6 A.M. They sit at the table, eat breakfast, drink coffee, gossip, and talk about world affairs. They leave by 7, and then the next group comes in. They leave by 8 or 8:30, then the last group comes in. They all come back for lunch, and if they come at night for dinner, they bring their families."

According to waitress Marietta, Bull Table members drink a lot of coffee, at least eight to ten cups apiece. In fact, the three-gallon coffee dispenser has to be refilled two or three times throughout the morning. "And whenever a new guy walks in, he has to refill everyone's cup," she says. "That's the rule."

The Bull Table, which seats about 14 to 16 people, has been around as long as Andy's Diner. The original owner, Andy Knopp, opened his first restaurant, the Country Diner, on Highway 87 sometime in the early fifties. Then he moved to Washington Street and renamed his business Andy's Diner. He started with one dining room and a counter with diner-style stools. Through the years, he expanded more. In 1991 Don and Mary Wise bought the place and have been running it ever since. Don, a train buff, added the miniature trains that run along tracks attached near the ceilings.

At noon, Andy's Diner fills up fast. Most customers order the lunch special, which comes with choice of meat, two vegetables, drink, and dessert. The extensive menu offers a little of everything—appetizers, salads, steaks, seafood, fried chicken, Mexican and German dishes, and sandwiches. A popular choice is Andy's Country Fried Steak, a 6-ounce, battered-and-fried steak served with cream gravy (better known as a chicken-fried steak). "We kept the 'country' part because of Andy's original restaurant," Don explains.

When I spotted a familiar-looking contraption perched on a shelf, I stepped over for a closer look and was hit with memories from my childhood. Called "Hi-Way Information by Travelog," it's a round cylinder encased in a plastic tube that twirls around on a spindle. Turn the knob, and you'll find the mileage from Fredericksburg to hundreds of exotic places, like Abilene, Marfa, Lufkin, Atlanta, and Miami (1,432 miles!). I remember spinning one of those as a kid. Like the notorious Bull Table, the Travelog has been around as long as the diner.

"People walk in and ask about it," Don says of the antique. "They remember it from past visits."

When you stop by Andy's for lunch next time, be sure and check out the Travelog and also the Bull Table in the front dining room. It's the extra long table that stands beneath the collection of cattle brands on the wall. You'll also see this thought-provoking little sign that says, "How do you expect to raise cattle when you just keep shootin' the bull?"

Bull Table regulars have managed to do both just fine, thank you very much.

Gettin' there: From Main Street (U.S. 290), turn south on Washington Street (Admiral Nimitz Museum is on the corner). Andy's Diner is less than a half mile down the street on the left.

Andy's Diner
413 S. Washington
Fredericksburg, TX 78624
830/997-3744

Stop by and see: One of the most awesome sights you'll ever see in Texas is Enchanted Rock, a huge pink granite dome located 18 miles north of Fredericksburg on RR 965. Yes, you can hike to the summit, provided you pay the entrance fee to Enchanted Rock State Natural Area.

Fresh German Potato Salad

Boil 3 pounds of potatoes in a pot of water until potatoes are soft. Peel the potatoes and cut into chunks.

Dressing:
2 cups vinegar

2 cups sugar
1 cup diced onions
1 cup diced bacon and grease
black pepper to taste

Mix the above ingredients in a pan and bring to a boil. Pour over potatoes while still hot. Mix gently and serve.

Fresh German Fried Potatoes

Bake one potato per person. Slice the potato in nice even slices, leaving the peel on. Grill the slices on a hot, flat-top grill or in a skillet in a little butter. When the potato slices are almost done (brown), add diced onions, red peppers, and bell peppers. Salt and pepper to taste.

Hunt

Hunt Store and Cafe
(1965)

The Hunt Store opened in 1949 and was at one time the only grocery store and meat market in western Kerr County. In 1965 local folks and summer campers encouraged the store owners to open a cafe so they didn't have to drive the 15 miles to Kerrville for something to eat.

Today, the Hunt Store, a rock-and-cedar building with a covered front porch, still supplies and feeds local residents along with summertime visitors and passersby on the highway. They stop to buy groceries as well as eat a meal in the cafe, located in back of the store. Customers especially enjoy one menu favorite, Bob's Cheeseburger (named for owner Bob Denison). The sandwich features a ⅓-pound choice beef patty served on a toasted bun with Monterey jack cheese, sauteed mushrooms and onions, and jalapeños on the side. The chicken salad sandwich is made with the cafe's slow-smoked chicken and served on a buttery croissant (white or wheat bread available, too). And ever heard of French tacos? You'll find them here. Though they may sound European, they're actually named for a customer, James French, who originated the recipe in 1972. The tacos come with your choice of a split beef patty or chicken breast on two flour tortillas, topped with lettuce, tomatoes, onions, and pickles.

Gettin' there: Hunt is located west of Kerrville on Texas 39.

Hunt Store
Highway 39
Hunt, TX 78024
830/238-4410

Stop by and see: Two miles west of Hunt on FM 1340 is the Texas version of Stonehenge, a massive monument built of stones in Wiltshire, England. The Hill Country replica is an exact three-quarter-scale model of the original stone circle. You'll also see several replicas of the solemn-faced statues found on Easter Island in the South Pacific.

Lampasas

Martin's Restaurant
(1952)

Martin's is another one of those Texas restaurants that hasn't changed much since it opened more than four decades ago.

The old built-in phone booth in a front corner has been there so long that owner Bennie Martin doubts the telephone companies even remember to whom it belongs. The cash register on the front counter was bought used in 1947 and is so heavy that it wasn't washed away in the 1957 Mother's Day flood (a line on the front door marks how high the water reached inside the building—nearly 6 feet). Raging waters, though, did sweep away the cafe's tables and chairs. Their replacements are still in use at Martin's, which reopened for business a month after the flood. The funky upholstered chairs get a lot of attention. "People are always wanting to buy them," Bennie says.

Delbert Martin, Bennie's father-in-law, started in the restaurant business back in '47 when he leased Jose's Cafe in Lampasas. In 1952 he opened his own place on Key Avenue and appropriately named it Martin's Restaurant. Bennie's husband, Gary, worked in the cafe as a teenager. As a young man, he followed in his dad's footsteps and worked at Wyatt's Cafeterias in Dallas and San Antonio. When Delbert died in 1965, Gary and Bennie assumed management of Martin's. Since suffering a massive heart attack, Gary has retired to take life easier.

Not so for a familiar face in the kitchen. Jerry Martinez has flipped eggs and rustled up lunch specials since Delbert's days. "What's the best part of the job?" asks Jerry, wiping his hands on the white apron tied around his waist. "Gettin' up in the morning." He grins mischievously, then adds, "People through the years get used to your cooking. I'm just glad I can still do it."

Most of the Jerry's fans are local folks who come in regularly. One is Sam, who claims a spot at a back table near the kitchen. "He sits in the same place morning and noon," Bennie confides. "The girls leave his table dirty from breakfast until he gets here at noon. That's so no one will sit at it."

Don't worry. There's plenty of other places to claim. Booths line up along one far wall, and smaller two-seater versions stand along a counter. Regular tables outfitted with those popular chairs are arranged in the main dining room and an adjoining one, too.

Bennie hopes to sell Martin's someday soon so she can retire. Hopefully, someone who cares about keeping the phone booth intact and the cash register in place will snap it right up.

Gettin' there: Martin's is located at the corner of Fifth and Key Avenues (U.S. 281).

Martin's Restaurant
801 S. Key Ave.
Lampasas, TX 76550
512/556-3362

Stop by and see: A great place to walk off lunch is the W.M. Brooke Park. Sidewalks parallel Sulphur Creek, and picnic tables overlook the water. There's also a single-span suspension bridge across the creek.

Canadian Cheese Soup

¼ cup butter
½ cup finely diced or grated onion
½ cup finely diced or grated carrots
½ cup finely diced or grated celery
¼ cup flour
1½ tablespoon cornstarch
1 quart chicken stock
2 cups cheese sauce
⅛ teaspoon baking soda
1 cup evaporated milk
salt, pepper, parsley

Melt butter in a large saucepan. Add onions, carrots, and celery; saute until soft. Add flour and cornstarch and cook until bubbly. Add stock slowly to make smooth sauce. Add cheese sauce and baking soda, stirring gently. Add milk and seasonings to taste. Serves 8.

Corn Chowder Soup

½ pound diced bacon
4 large, thinly sliced onions
½ #10 can (6½ to 7¼ pounds) cream-style corn
4 large diced, raw potatoes
¼ #10 can diced tomatoes
1½ gallons chicken stock
1 12-ounce can evaporated milk
salt, pepper, sugar

Cook diced bacon. Add onions and saute until soft. Add corn, potatoes, tomatoes, and chicken stock. Cook until potatoes are tender. Season to taste with salt and pepper and a dash of sugar. Add milk. Serves 40.

Lemon Chess Pie

2 cups sugar
1 tablespoon flour
1 tablespoon cornmeal
dash salt
$\frac{1}{4}$ cup melted butter
$\frac{1}{4}$ cup milk
$\frac{1}{4}$ cup lemon juice
4 eggs

Combine sugar, flour, cornmeal, and salt. Add the melted butter, lemon juice, and milk; mix well. Add the eggs, one at a time, beating well after each addition. Pour into an unbaked 9-inch pie shell, and bake at 350 degrees for 50 minutes or until set.

Marble Falls

Blue Bonnet Cafe
(1929)

My wristwatch reads not quite 11 A.M., and yet the parking lot at the Blue Bonnet is already full. I walk in through the back entrance and wait for a table. Most are occupied. But it isn't long before a cheery waitress whisks the crumbs away at a booth, and I slide in.

Be prepared to wait your turn for a granite-topped table at the Blue Bonnet.

"This is a real busy place," confirms long-time owner John Kemper. "On a Saturday, we feed an average of 2,000 people, and a thousand on Sunday. The rest of the week it's about 800 people a day." The cafe only seats 120 customers; hence the wait at peak times.

The Blue Bonnet—named for the woman's hat and not the famous Texas flower—has been feeding folks since 1929 when it was located on Main Street. Through the years, several owners have run the restaurant, which moved to the highway in '46. Since 1981 John and his wife, Belinda, have kept the Marble Falls tradition going. His late father, George Kemper, crafted the striking countertops and tabletops, made of granite from Marble Falls and all over the world (Canada, Norway, North Dakota, and Georgia).

Breakfast here is served 'round the clock. You can order a traditional morning meal of eggs with bacon, ham, or sausage, served alongside of hash browns or grits, Texas toast, biscuits, or thin toast. Heartier appetites can order eggs with a chicken-fried steak or a 6-ounce top sirloin. And omelette lovers, rejoice—the Blue Bonnet's menu lists eight different kinds, such as plain, cheese, onion, Western, and Spanish style. A word of advice: if you're not that hungry, DON'T order a cinnamon roll or else ask for a bag. From the looks of the morning's batch stuffed into a display box on the counter, the giant homemade puffs of sweetness looked like they might feed three or four people.

From 11 A.M. 'til closing, daily specials feature more than ten entrees, including chicken-fried steak (the best seller at lunch), sirloin steak, grilled liver and onion, chicken and dumplings (Tuesdays only), pot roast, and turkey and dressing (every other Sunday). The plates come with homemade yeast rolls and your choice of three side dishes: soup, salad, mashed potatoes, French fries, and six different veggies—Italian cut green beans, buttered leaf spinach, fried okra (my personal favorite), pinto beans, mini cob corn, and buttered baby carrots.

"We're a real Texas cafe," John says. "We do all our own baking. We average 50 to 75 pies a day, and 100 to 150 on Saturday. Our coconut meringue is the best seller. People also like the coconut cream."

Both local folks and travelers frequent the Blue Bonnet, one of Marble Fall's hotspots for coffee breaks. Over the years, many famous people have stopped by the cafe to eat, too. John can't remember them all, but a few names come to mind when he's asked, like Gov. George W. Bush, Willie Nelson, Roger Staubach, and Lyle Lovett.

On extra busy days when the waiting line is long, John sometimes asks people if they'd mind sharing their table. "One time I asked two older ladies if I could seat two gentlemen at their table, and they said yes," he recalls. "They all got to talking, and they realized they had grown up together in Brownwood. They started reminiscing, and one man said he remembered a redheaded girl who babysat him as a child. And one of the women then said, 'Why, that was me!'"

Every day's an adventure at the Blue Bonnet Cafe in Marble Falls.

Gettin' there: The Blue Bonnet is located a few feet off U.S. 281 on the south side of town.

Blue Bonnet Cafe
211 Hwy. 281
Marble Falls, TX 78654
830/693-2344

Stop by and see: That beautiful Victorian home near the Blue Bonnet was built in 1887 by the founder of Marble Falls, Adam

Rankin Johnson. Owner Wilburn Wall grew up in the three-story house and restored it in 1983. Today his stately home is a lovely bed-and-breakfast inn, the Liberty Hall Historic Guest Haus.

The following recipes are from Belinda Kemper's cookbook *What's Cooking at the Blue Bonnet Cafe.* Sorry, the book doesn't include Belinda's recipe for chicken-fried steak.

This special is served every Wednesday.

Blue Bonnet's Meat Loaf

2 pounds lean hamburger meat
I slice white bread, torn into pieces or ¼ cup cracker crumbs
2 eggs, beaten
½ cup chopped onion
½ cup chopped green bell pepper
I tablespoon A-I Sauce
I teaspoon celery salt
½ teaspoon pepper
3 slices bacon

Mix above ingredients, except bacon. Form into a loaf and place on baking sheet. Cover with strips of bacon. Bake at 350 degrees for 45 minutes. Pour on sauce and bake 10 to 15 minutes longer.

Sauce:
½ cup chopped onion
½ cup chopped celery
I (15-ounce) can stewed tomatoes, chopped
I or 2 tablespoons beef base
I cup water
I teaspoon garlic powder

Boil above ingredients until tender and mixture is thick. (Add some flour if you need to thicken.)

My friend and fellow writer Paris Permenter and I order this every time we meet for lunch at the Blue Bonnet.

Blue Bonnet's Spinach Salad with Hot Bacon Dressing

I package fresh spinach, washed, torn, stems removed
2 tomatoes, chopped into small pieces

4 hard-boiled eggs, chopped up
croutons

Place spinach on four large plates. On top, sprinkle chopped tomatoes and chopped boiled egg. Pour hot bacon dressing on top and gently toss. Top with croutons.

Hot bacon dressing:
8 slices bacon
4 tablespoons cider vinegar
4 tablespoons water
2 tablespoons sugar
2 eggs, beaten

Cook bacon in a large skillet until crisp; remove bacon, crumble and set aside. Add vinegar, water, and sugar to bacon drippings; bring to a boil. Remove from heat. Gradually stir $\frac{1}{4}$ of hot mixture into beaten eggs; add egg mixture to skillet, stirring constantly, until thickened. Stir in bacon. Makes four main course servings.

Blue Bonnet's Corn Bread Muffins

1 $\frac{1}{2}$ cups flour
1 $\frac{1}{2}$ cups cornmeal
$\frac{1}{8}$ cup sugar
$\frac{1}{8}$ cup baking powder
2 teaspoons salt
$\frac{1}{8}$ cup melted margarine
1 egg, beaten
3 cups milk

Combine dry ingredients; add melted margarine, beaten egg, and milk. Mix until dry ingredients are moistened, being careful not to overmix. Pour batter into greased muffin tins. Bake in moderate oven until done.

This pie is good stuff—I promise.

Blue Bonnet's Fudge Pie

6 ounces butter, melted
3 (1-ounce) squares unsweetened chocolate, melted
$\frac{1}{2}$ cup flour
3 eggs, beaten
1 $\frac{1}{2}$ cups sugar
2 teaspoons vanilla
$\frac{1}{2}$ teaspoon salt

Melt chocolate and butter together over low heat. Mix remaining ingredients in a separate bowl. Gradually pour in melted chocolate and butter while mixing. When mixture is well beaten, pour into an unbaked 9-inch pie shell. Bake at 325 degrees for 35 to 40 minutes.

Michel's Drug Store
(1891)

As a light rain dampens Main Street, two women out for the afternoon duck into Michel's Drug Store in downtown Marble Falls and plop down at a dainty ice cream table.

"What would you ladies like to order?" asks the woman behind the old-fashioned soda fountain.

"How about a Coke and a 400?" replies one.

"What's that?" wonders the woman, crinkling her forehead in puzzlement. "I've never heard of that one."

"A 400 is chocolate milk with ice," the customer explains.

Working quickly and efficiently, the soda jerk squirts a bit of chocolate into one glass and syrup into another. Then she adds milk and soda. A few moments later, she presents the women with a Coke and—voila—a 400.

Besides touting the area's only soda fountain, Michel's (pronounced like the name Michelle) Drug Store has another claim to fame.

"We haven't proven it, but we claim to be the longest continuously operated family drugstore in the state," boasts Douglas Michel Jr. "And no one's ever proven us wrong."

Douglas's great-grandfather, German immigrant Ernst Gustav Michel, opened the drugstore in 1891 and rebuilt it in 1927 after a blaze set by a robber destroyed the west side of Main Street. E.G. died in 1930 and his son E.G. Jr. ran the store until he was killed in an auto accident in 1935. That same year, a second son—Gus Michel—shut down his pharmacy in San Benito and moved to Marble Falls to take over the struggling family business. He worked at the drugstore until his death in 1976.

Douglas Sr., an Army chaplain, accepted the store's reins in 1978 at his mother's urging. In 1980 Doug Jr. became the drugstore's pharmacist.

In addition to cherry Cokes and malts, the drugstore also serves lunch from 11 A.M. to 2 P.M. A menu, handwritten on a Coca-Cola chalkboard, lists the day's offerings of sandwiches and salads. A selection of antiques, jewelry, toiletries, cards, candy, and other gift items entice visitors to browse while they wait for their lunch.

Gettin' there: From U.S. 281, turn west on Second or Third Street. Main Street is one block from the highway.

Michel's Drug Store
216 Main St.
Marble Falls, TX 78654
830/693-4250

Stop by and see: During the 1880s a natural phenomenon called Granite Mountain secured Marble Falls' place in Texas history. In exchange for a rail connection with Austin, owners of the 866-foot dome of pink granite provided the beautiful stone used to build the state's capitol. Today a company called Cold Springs Texas Granite still quarries at Granite Mountain, which can be seen from a roadside park on RR 1431. A granite monument marks the site.

Some Texas trivia: A historical marker on a hillside south of the Colorado River bridge commemorates Oscar J. Fox, composer of the famous song, "The Hills of Home." From this scenic overlook near U.S. 281, Fox was inspired to write his popular song in 1925.

New Braunfels

Krause's Cafe
(1938)

Prince Carl Solms-Braunfels in March 1845 incorporated the city of New Braunfels and christened it in honor of his estate on the Lahn River in western Germany, Braunfels. Within a decade, the settlement of more than 300 Germans grew into a major manufacturing center along the Austin-San Antonio road. The point of this mini lesson in history: if you're ever in New Braunfels, EAT GERMAN FOOD!

One of the best places to eat sauerbraten, sausage, and schnitzel is Krause's Cafe on South Castell Avenue. The history at this popular restaurant goes back to 1938 when the original owner, Gene Krause, opened a tavern on the plaza and called it Gene's Place. In 1948 he moved the business to its present location. A few years later he expanded his menu and changed the name to Krause's Cafe. The Krause family ran the cafe until 1998 when Glenn and Rebecca bought it.

"Our goal then, as now, is to keep the good food that was handed down through the family and to add new items as well," Rebecca says. "We are well known for our home-cooked meals, authentic German food, huge charbroiled hamburgers, and barbecue. In the winter months, we make homemade tamales, which everyone in town buys for the holidays."

Besides German cuisine, Krause's also claims a bit of fame in the sweets department. Every day the cafe bakes more than 20 varieties of cakes, pies, and cheesecakes.

Gettin' there: From I-35, take exit 187 (Seguin Avenue) and go west. That is a right turn if you are headed south on I-35, left turn if you are headed north on I-35. On Seguin Avenue, go four traffic lights (about 1 mile) to Coll Street and turn left. Go one block to Castell Street and turn right. Krause's is about one block on the left.

Krause's Cafe
148 S. Castell Ave.
New Braunfels, TX 78130
830/625-7581

Stop by and see: Beautiful Landa Park encircles the springs that head the Comal River, the state's shortest river (2.5 miles). Spring-fed pools, picnic sites, hiking, and a miniature train make this city park an ideal place to spend an afternoon.

Sauerbraten

1 10-pound inside round roast
2¾ cups water
1½ cups red wine vinegar

Place roast, water, and vinegar in a roaster and cover. Let cook in oven at 375 degrees for 1½ hours. Then add ingredients below to the roaster and cook until done (about 2 hours).

5⅓ cups water
1⅓ cups red wine vinegar
1⅓ cups granulated sugar
⅛ cup whole cloves
1 large onion, cut up
⅓ box of ginger snaps (we use the 1-pound box)
4 bay leaves

After roast is done, remove and slice thinly. Strain juices from roaster and thicken with cornstarch and water mixture. Cook to a boil, then reduce heat until desired thickness is achieved.

New Braunfels Smokehouse Restaurant
(1945)

The New Braunfels Smokehouse just off the interstate is another one of those local German-style institutions you have to visit if you're ever in the area.

In 1943 a man by the name of R.K. Dunbar bought the South Texas Ice Company and a couple of years later turned the building into a locker plant. There, farmers and ranchers stored their hams, turkeys, and bacon and also had them smoked. Soon the locker plant began smoking and selling its own meat. In 1952 Dunbar and his family built a "tasting room" and retail shop on Highway 81 to sell their hickory-smoked products. The tasting room soon became a restaurant. Business boomed, and the Dunbars expanded the restaurant to keep up with customers and meat orders. In 1967 the Dunbars moved the building to its present location, a 4.5-acre tract of land blessed with giant oak trees and a natural spring. They also built more dining rooms and expanded the menu.

It wasn't long before out-of-town customers, smitten with the Smokehouse's delicious meats, asked if the restaurant could ship them. The Dunbars obliged, and a sizable mail-order business developed. In 1969 Smokehouse shipments went from in-state only to nationwide. Today the business mails out more than 600,000 catalogs a year and serves more than 100,000 customers across the country. Products include hickory-smoked turkeys, hams, jerky, bacon, pork chops, chicken, and sausage, all processed at the Smokehouse's plant in New Braunfels. The catalog also offers pecan pies, pecan brownies, divinity, preserves, cheeses, and mustards.

After all these years, the Smokehouse is still family owned. Susan Dunbar Snyder and her husband, Dudley Snyder, own and operate the multi-faceted business, which has expanded to include two restaurants in San Antonio.

Speaking of restaurants and food, the Smokehouse menu features lots of good fixin's, many of them served German style. Breakfast fare includes eggs, breakfast tacos, biscuits with sausage gravy, pancakes, Belgian waffles, and French toast. At lunch during the week, customers can order the daily special, which could be—depending on the day of the week—a chopped barbecue beef sandwich, smoked sausage and sauerkraut, chicken-fried steak, bratwurst or barbecue beef brisket. Under "Appetizers," there's the Wunderbar, an assortment of Smokehouse meats and cheeses. Other tasty appetizers are hot sausage links with mustard and bread, and Bismarkian sausage served with cheese, crackers, and mustard. For light appetites, four kinds of soups (German potato, vegetable beef, split pea, and tortilla), salads, and oodles of sandwiches (from hot ham to turkey dijon) make the decisions tough. Hungrier folks will go for a Smokehouse specialty (such as smoked pork chops, a grilled chicken breast, chicken and dumplings, or a sausage platter) or Smokehouse dinner (barbecue brisket, ribs, chicken, and sausage, all served with pintos, German potato salad, and a tossed salad).

Meals at the Smokehouse are always followed by a leisurely browse through the restaurant's retail shop, where customers can buy Smokehouse meats, cookbooks, gourmet foods, and other gift items.

Gettin' there: From I-35, take Exit 189 and turn west onto Texas 46. You'll see the Smokehouse on the left side of the street.

New Braunfels Smokehouse Restaurant
146 Highway 46 East
P.O. Box 311159
New Braunfels, TX 78131
830/625-2416
Mail order: 800/537-6932

Other locations:
6450 N. New Braunfels Ave. (Sunset Ridge Shopping Center)
San Antonio, TX 78209
210/826-6008

16607 Huebner Rd. (Deerfield Crossing Shopping Center)
San Antonio, TX 78248
210/493-9626
Website: www.nbsmokehouse.com

Stop by and see: Check out the little town of Gruene (pronounced "green") on the Guadalupe River off North Loop 337. Historic homes, lots of shops, an art gallery, winery, and a rustic dance hall line two main streets.

Smokehouse Cranberry Salad
2 packages (3 ounces each) cherry gelatin
2 cups boiling water
1 16-ounce whole-berry cranberry sauce
1 7-ounce can crushed pineapple, well drained
$\frac{1}{4}$ cup finely chopped celery
mayonnaise for garnish
fresh cranberries for garnish

Dissolve gelatin in hot water. Let cool slightly. Add cranberry sauce, drained pineapple, and celery. Pour into 6-cup mold or 8 to 10 individual gelatin molds. Chill overnight or until firm. Top each portion with small dollop of mayonnaise. Garnish with fresh cranberries, if desired.

Smokehouse Turkey and Bacon Salad
4 thick slices Smokehouse Bacon, cooked crisp and crumbled in small pieces ($\frac{1}{2}$ cup)

2 cups Smokehouse Smoked Turkey, cut in bite-sized pieces
¾ cup chopped celery
¼ cup sweet pickle relish
¼ to ½ cup homemade or good quality purchased mayonnaise (no substitutes)

Combine bacon, turkey, and celery. Toss gently. Add relish. Add just enough mayonnaise to lightly coat mixture but not overpower the taste. This makes a delicious filling for a sandwich or a stuffed tomato. Serves six to eight people.

Smokehouse Potato Soup

4 large Idaho potatoes
3 tablespoons butter
½ cup chopped onion
7 cups water
2 teaspoons salt, to taste
I teaspoon black pepper
I cup finely chopped dried beef

Wash, peel, and cut potatoes into small cubes or thin slices. Set aside. Melt butter in a large stock pot over medium heat. Add onion and saute until tender. Add water, salt, and black pepper. Bring to a boil, reduce heat to medium-low, and stirring occasionally, simmer 45 to 55 minutes or until potatoes are soft.

Using a wooden spoon, stir soup, lightly mashing the potatoes, until the mixture is well blended and thick. Place in serving bowls and top with heaping tablespoons of dried beef. Serve. Makes about 7 cups.

Waco

Elite Cafe
(1941)

Anyone who's traveled the highway between Dallas and Austin knows the Elite Cafe. This architectural landmark sits "on the circle," the infamous traffic hub built in 1934 where five high-ways converged on the outskirts of Waco.

Today, cafe t-shirts and menus, emblazoned with "I sur-vived The Circle," pay tribute to the outdated means of directing traffic. If you've driven around the circle on your way to the Elite, then you know how dizzying it can be. Merging onto the circle with oncoming traffic reminds me of jumping rope with girlfriends as a kid. While they turned the rope, I had to time my entry and initial jump PERFECTLY or else I'd mess up the rhythm. The traffic circle in Waco and another one I remember in Henderson, Texas, work pretty much on the jump-rope premise. In the years since Interstate 35 was con-structed, some folks tried to get rid of The Circle, but local circle enthusiasts prevailed and preserved it for your driving pleasure. Everyone needs to experience The Circle at least once.

But I digress. Getting back to the Elite.... The first Elite Cafe opened in 1919 on Austin Avenue in downtown Waco and the next year was purchased by the Colias family from Sparta, Greece. In 1941 Mike and George Colias opened a second Elite Cafe on the traffic circle in the "suburbs" of Waco. Initially, the restaurant offered curb service with little indoor seating, but that changed when the brothers decided to enlarge the build-ing. The pair, great entrepreneurs for their time, in 1923 boasted the first mechanical refrigerator in a Waco restaurant and in 1935 the first air-conditioned restaurant in town. In 1965 they closed their downtown location. In 1985 the Colias family sold the Elite to David Tinsley, who heavily restored the cafe and kept its history going. He's since sold the landmark, and the new owners are just as dedicated to preserving the Elite.

Even the domed ceiling inside the front entrance honors The Circle. In the rotunda, look up, and you'll see a yellow neon light outlining the circular ceiling. Below on the curving wall hang old color-tinted photos of the Elite, the next-door Health Camp burger stand, and other Waco sites. Photographs from the city's past hang throughout the restaurant. Other vestiges from the past sit on the tile floor near the entrance—an old Hobart floor mixer (circa 1940) and a dough press, both once used in the cafe's kitchen.

And what's on the menu? Everything you can imagine a serious cafe would serve, like hamburgers and onion rings. The cafe's specialty, naturally, is a Circle chicken-fried steak, a 4- or 8-ounce cutlet hand breaded in homemade batter and topped with peppered cream gravy. Appetizers, soups, salads, shrimp and catfish, steaks, fajitas, and chicken entrees round out the menu's other offerings.

On your way out, stop a minute and read the Texas Historical Marker posted outside the front door. The Elite Cafe, one of only a few in the state, received the marker in 1996.

Gettin' there: From I-35, take the Valley Mills Drive exit, turn east, and head for the tall, round "Waco Elite Cafe" sign. You're on your own at The Circle. Best of luck.

Elite Cafe
2132 S. Valley Mills Dr.
Waco, TX 76706
254/754-4941

Stop by and see: Waco, a spur on the Chisholm Trail, enjoyed its first economic boom after the Waco Bridge Company in 1870 constructed a suspension bridge across the Brazos River. The company later built the Brooklyn Bridge, using the Waco bridge as a model. Townsfolk, ranchers, and cattle all frequented the Waco bridge, a graceful landmark open these days only to pedestrians and bicyclists.

Here's a tasty salad dressing. Makes a lot.

Elite Dressing

3 quarts mayonnaise
I quart tomato soup
3 tablespoons granulated garlic
3 tablespoons white vinegar
3 tablespoons salad mustard
I teaspoon Tabasco sauce
I teaspoon Worcestershire sauce
¼ cup paprika

Procedure: Combine mayonnaise and tomato soup. Add the additional ingredients using wire whip until thoroughly mixed. Chill and serve. Yields I gallon.

Texas Historical Marker Elite Cafe

The first Elite Cafe opened in downtown Waco in 1919 and was acquired by the Greek immigrant Colias family in 1920. The Colias brothers opened this Elite Cafe in 1941 on "The Circle," a traffic hub built on Waco's suburban edge in the early 1930s. A highly recognized local landmark, and one of the best remaining regional examples of mid-twentieth-century roadside architecture, the building exhibits a distinctive Spanish colonial style popular in the southwest.

Welfare

Po-Po Family Restaurant
(1938)

Every February, Carol Hood tackles a massive project at the Po-Po Family Restaurant off Interstate 10 north of Boerne.

She washes dishes.

So what? Well, just imagine dunking more than 1,500 dishes in soapy water, and the mental picture puts the woman's task a bit more in perspective. What's more, the countless numbers of commemorative plates hang on the restaurant's walls, so they have to be carefully removed and then rehung. But Carol doesn't mind the work. She's been doing it ever since she was a child.

"Every June, my grandparents would close the restaurant for the month and then travel," recalls Carol, today assistant manager at the popular Hill Country eatery. "But before we left, we had to wash the plates. The sooner we got them all done, the sooner we could leave on vacation."

"Back then, I did it 'cause I had to," she adds. "Now I do it 'cause I like to."

Luther and Marie Burgon, Carol's grandparents, in 1950 bought the cafe (named by a previous owner for the Mexican volcano, Popocátepetl) and limestone building, originally built almost 70 years ago. As souvenirs from their travels, they'd buy plates and hang them in their cafe. Customers contributed, too, and, as the years passed, the plate collection ballooned to 1,000.

In 1983 Jerry and Jenny Tilley and their son, David, bought Po-Po's and inherited approximately 700 of the original plates. To this day, customers still faithfully add to the collection, which numbers 1,541. Ranging from ceramic to pewter, Elvis Presley to John F. Kennedy, the colorful and unusual plates hang nearly rim to rim on walls and ceiling beams. "We average one donated plate a week," Jerry says. "People Fed Ex or mail them."

Though the huge assortment of commemorative plates attracts a lot of attention, it's the plain white dinner plates piled high with fried chicken, steaks, and seafood that draw people from across Texas and even the country to this out-of-the-way cafe.

"The amount of people who have heard about this place never ceases to amaze me," Jerry says. "I've heard people say they were hunting in Colorado or were at a zoo in Philadelphia and heard about the food at Po-Po's."

The restaurant's reputation for good food is deserved. Crisply fried and blanketed with cream gravy, the chicken-fried steak here is a top seller. Other house specialties are the jumbo butterflied shrimp, fried catfish, and steaks. Entrees come with choice of two: cup of soup (the chicken gumbo is another specialty), salad, coleslaw, rice pilaf, baked potato, authentic mashed potatoes, steak fries, French fries, or a vegetable.

Jerry's baby back pork ribs hit the menu Fridays and Saturdays, and Sundays are turkey-and-dressing day, another customer favorite served with giblet gravy, mashed potatoes, green beans, cranberry sauce, and the cafe's homemade biscuits. All-you-can-eat plates of fried shrimp, boiled shrimp, fried chicken, and/or fried catfish are available Monday through Thursday.

And the grand finale to a meal at Po-Po's? How about a sumptuous Popocateletl special dessert? That's a homemade brownie topped with Blue Bell ice cream, chocolate sauce, whipped cream, and a plump cherry on top.

Gettin' there: From Boerne, head north on Interstate 10 and exit Welfare/FM 289. Po-Po Family Restaurant is located a half mile north. Reservations are recommended.

Po-Po Family Restaurant
435 NE I-10 Access Rd.
Boerne, TX 78006
830/537-4194

Po-Po Family Restaurant's Butterflied Fried Shrimp

32 (about 2 pounds) jumbo shrimp

Wet batter:
2 cups whole milk
½ egg (beat egg in small cup, add half to batter)
¾ teaspoon salt
¼ teaspoon white pepper

Dry batter:
2 cups extra-fine cracker meal
⅔ cup "hard-wheat" (bread) flour
¾ teaspoon self-rising biscuit mix
2 teaspoons lemon Jello powder (dry)
2 teaspoons salt
1 teaspoon white pepper
½ teaspoon red pepper (optional)
peanut oil for frying

Prepare shrimp: Peel shell, leaving it intact on the tail. Devein, then butterfly the shrimp by cutting along the inside curve, being careful not to cut all the way through. This allows the two halves to open like a butterfly's wings.

In a bowl, combine the ingredients for the wet batter. In a second bowl, mix the ingredients for the dry batter and stir well. Heat oil in a deep pan to 325 degrees. Holding shrimp by the tail, dip in wet batter, then in dry. Shake off excess, then drop into the hot oil and cook until golden brown, about 1 minute. Do not drop too many in at one time. Remove with a slotted spoon and drain on a paper towel. Serves four.

Old World Deli German Potato Salad

4 pounds red potatoes
½ to 1 medium onion, chopped
2-3 slices bacon, crisply fried and crumbled
1 tablespoon chopped fresh parsley
1 tablespoon salt
½ teaspoon black pepper
⅓ cup white vinegar
1 tablespoon water
½ cup vegetable oil
⅓ cup beef stock
½-1 teaspoon sugar

Boil potatoes until almost done. Remove skins, slice thinly ($\frac{1}{8}$ to $\frac{1}{4}$ inches thick), and place in baking pan. Mix other ingredients. Toss over warm potatoes to coat. Bake 275 degrees about 30-40 minutes. Serve.

Sweet Potato Casserole

I large can yams, drained and mashed
2 eggs, beaten
I teaspoon salt
$\frac{2}{3}$ cup milk with $\frac{1}{2}$ teaspoon baking powder
I teaspoon vanilla
$\frac{1}{4}$ cup soft butter

Mix and bake at 350 degrees for 20 minutes. Spread with topping.

Topping:
I cup pecans mixed with $\frac{1}{3}$ cup flour
I cup brown sugar
$\frac{1}{4}$ cup butter, melted

Mix together and spread over yams. Bake 20 minutes more. Serve.

Wimberley

Burger Barn

(about 1968)

Folks around this Hill Country hamlet on the Blanco River can't exactly recall the year the Burger Barn opened on Ranch Road 12. But I can remember the original one-room building, covered with wood and painted rusty red, from the time I visited there as a child, and I'm forty-something (OK, I'll be brutally honest. I was born in '59). My grandfather, Mose Smith, retired in Wimberley during the fifties, and we'd go see him several times a year. Now and then, we'd order take-out from the

Burger Barn, which, if my memory serves me, closed during the winter months.

Three decades later, the Burger Barn has grown to include a small dining room that seats a faithful following of customers. They come for coffee in the morning and breakfast, too, such as eggs, pancakes, biscuits, burritos, grits, and gravy. Posted on the wall, the lunch menu lists burgers, steak sandwiches, ham sandwiches, corn dogs, chili, enchiladas, fries, onion rings, and salad. A few other signs hang on the wall, such as one that reads "If you don't want it to get out, don't tell it here."

Another one: "In a small town there may not be much to see, but what you hear sure makes up for it."

Ain't that the truth!

Gettin' there: The Burger Barn is located on Ranch Road 12, just south of downtown.

Burger Barn
13601 Ranch Rd. 12
Wimberley, TX 78676
512/847-9276

Stop by and see: A busy but fun time to visit Wimberley is the first Saturday of the month, April through December. That's when the Wimberley Lion's Club Market Day, located northeast of town on Ranch Road 2325, brings vendors and buyers together for a day-long shopping bonanza.

Peach Cobbler

2 cans (16-ounces) peaches
2 cups flour
½ cup butter
1 cup sugar
1 tablespoon cinnamon

Place peaches in a 4-quart pot with enough water to fill pot. Bring to a boil. Mix flour with melted butter until it reaches a pasty consistency. Pour into the peach and water mixture. Add ¾ cup sugar and ½ tablespoon cinnamon. Make two pie crusts (or use frozen). Line a 9x13-inch baking dish with one crust. Pour mixture over crust; top with second crust. Mix remaining sugar and cinnamon together; sprinkle over crust. Cut slits into crust. Slice 4 to 5 tablespoons of margarine or butter on top. Bake 325 degrees for 30 to 45 minutes.

Charles' Frijoles a la Charra

2 pounds dry pinto beans
6 slices bacon (or ham hock)
¼ ounce salt
¼ ounce cumin
¼ ounce pepper
1 garlic clove
1 bunch cilantro
1 onion, diced
2 tomatoes, diced
2 jalapeños, diced

Boil beans, bacon, and seasonings until cooked. About 20 minutes before serving, add vegetables and bring to a boil.

Other old-time restaurants:

Abbott
Turkey Shop & Cafeteria (1966)
I-35
Abbott, TX 76621
254/582-2015

Austin
Cisco's Restaurant and Bakery (1929)
1511 E. Sixth St.
Austin, TX 78702
512/478-2420

Frisco Shop (1952)
5819 Burnet Rd.
Austin, TX 78756
512/459-6279

The Tavern (1912)
922 W. 12th St.
Austin, TX 78703
512/474-7496

Ballinger
Texas Grill (1950)
700 Hutchins Ave.
Ballinger, TX 76821
915/365-3314

Elgin
City Cafe (1910)
19 N. Main St.
Elgin, TX 78621
512/281-3663

Kerrville
Cowboy Steak House (1977)
416 Main St.
Kerrville, TX 78028
830/896-5688

New Braunfels
Oma's Haus Restaurant (1977)
P.O. Box 310667
New Braunfels, TX 78131
830/625-3280

Waco
Health Camp (1949)
2132 S. Valley Mills Dr.
Waco, TX 76706
254/752-2081

West
Sulak's Cafe (1923)
208 N. Main St.
West, TX 76691
254/826-7791

And one you've never heard of...

Somewhere in Texas, USA

Rodgers' Restaurant
(1981)

OK. This place doesn't meet my criteria for being "old." But in 2001 it will turn 20. And I can promise you that by the time it does close its doors for good, the Rodgers' Restaurant will have racked up many more decades. The good Lord willin', that is.

In case you haven't figured it out, Rodgers' Restaurant occupies the kitchen and dining room of our home. My husband, Terry (a state park superintendent), and I met in 1978 through our work. At the time, he was managing a Nueces County park in Corpus Christi, and I was the summer editor of the *Western Star* (which later merged with the Robstown newspaper and became the *Nueces County Record-Star*). Our friendship blossomed, and we married in 1981. Poor ol' Zardoz, Terry's faithful German shepherd, had to move out when I moved into the tiny residence at Hazel Bazemore Park. Terry's work with the Texas Parks and Wildlife Department later transferred us to state parks in Austin, Tatum (East Texas), and Blanco, where we've lived for the past decade.

During the course of our married life, we've discovered the joys of cooking meals and having guests for dinner, the warmth and fun of sharing conversation, smiles, laughs, and, yes, good food. Our children, Patrick and Lindsey, have met people from all walks of life, many of whom I've written about within the pages of our local newspaper, the *Blanco County News*. For instance, Cyril Nevelow, a crusty old gentleman who became a dear friend of mine, came to dinner once. At the table, he told a few colorful stories, using some colorful language. Laughing along with him, I decided that accepting and loving people as they are was the greater lesson for our children. My colleague, reporter Mark Holan (who's since moved on to bigger newspapers), shared meals with us often and seemed to appreciate being a part of a family. Other special friends, like Mark Malone, Teresa Thomas, Elizabeth Gallagher, Larry Fair, and our dear friends Rusty and Bret Adams (along with their kids—Allysson, Bradon, and Caleta), have blessed the circle of love within our home.

People like Mark and Larry who visit often go straight for the beige-colored guest book we keep on an oak cabinet near the front door. They know to sign their name and address, the date, and, if they're in the mood, a witty comment or two. My personal favorite is one penned by Bruce Bunn, Terry's former boss, back in '88: "Clean restrooms and NO litter!"

This spiral-bound book of ours holds so many, many memories of friends and family members. Some have since passed on. Others we've lost touch with. A few come by regularly to eat supper. No matter the frequency of their visits, we'll always have their signatures to remind us of their time with us. Flip through the pages, and you'll find the shaky signatures of our late grandparents, the firm ones of Terry's mother, Alice Rodgers, who died unexpectedly in 1998, the scrawled handwriting of college friends we rarely see any more, the familiar autographs of dear friends from Blanco and those from as far away as Miami (we love you, John, Glenda and Lindsay Wolin) . . . and also the john hancock of a troubled cowboy by the name of Larry who came to supper once, raved about our roasted rabbit and rosemary rolls, and then a few months later shot himself. I miss him.

Rosemary rolls, French bread, biscuits, chocolate chip cookies—they're all part of my recipe repertoire. I bake them so often that I don't even use the recipes any more. I finally learned to buy flour in 25-pound bags and chocolate chips in 10-pounders. Just cheaper and easier that way.

Not to slight Terry, he's become an accomplished cook in the kitchen himself. A skilled hunter and outdoor enthusiast, he provides our family every fall with venison, turkey, and wild hog, which he butchers and packages for the freezer (I let him have ALL that messy fun). He makes his own jerky (he and the kids fight over that stuff) and grinds his own sausage. Often, Terry cooks supper, too, something I truly appreciate. Just say the word, and he can cook up a mean pot of carne guisada or potato soup. He also enjoys barbecuing steaks on my grandfather's old steel pit, and every Christmas he smokes a turkey for our family dinner (I haven't cooked one YET in all our years of marriage). I think I'm going to hang onto him.

So after more than a year's worth of work, I'm done with this book. I hope you've enjoyed learning about our state's rich and plentiful number of well-established restaurants. If there's anything you'd like to share about one you've visited that I missed (and trust me, there's many more old-time restaurants to go) or have feedback on this book, please drop me a card or an email. And by the way, if you have any questions about spiders, I'm your woman. I have a very good reference library on spiders and an extensive (self-taught) knowledge about them. In fact, I keep a few live ones in jars at my desk.

But that's another book. And I've already started writing it.

Rodgers' Restaurant
P.O. Box 493
Blanco, TX 78606
sherylsr@moment.net

Patrick's good friend Cody Brooks loves me only for my cookies.

Chocolate Chip Cookies
1 stick margarine, softened
2 eggs
¾ cup sugar
¾ cup brown sugar
½ cup shortening
1 teaspoon vanilla
3 cups flour
1 teaspoon salt
1 teaspoon baking soda
1 cup chocolate chips

Blend margarine with sugars and eggs. Beat in the shortening and vanilla. Mix in 1 cup of flour, then add the salt and soda. Mix in rest of flour and chocolate chips. Drop by teaspoonfuls on ungreased baking sheet. Bake at 375 degrees for 9 to 11 minutes. Makes approximately 4 dozen cookies.

Once upon a time, a cowboy poet by the name of Bill McKay asked for my hand in marriage (my husband was standing right next to me!) just so he could eat my biscuits every morning. He and Terry are still good friends. This is a true story.

Marriage Proposal Biscuits

4½ teaspoons yeast
½ cup warm water
5 cups flour
2 teaspoons salt
2 teaspoons baking powder
1 teaspoon baking soda
2 tablespoons sugar
1 cup shortening
2 cups buttermilk

The night before: Dissolve yeast in water; set aside. In a medium-sized bowl and using a spoon, mix together flour, salt, baking powder, soda, and sugar. With a fork, cut in shortening. Stir in yeast mixture. Then pour in buttermilk and mix. Wrap bowl with plastic wrap and refrigerate overnight.

The next morning: Take half of dough and lightly knead. Roll out ½ inch thick and cut out biscuits. Place on ungreased baking sheet. Do the same with the other half of dough. Allow biscuits to rise half an hour or so. Bake at 400 degrees for 12 to 15 minutes. Makes about 3 dozen biscuits. They also taste great with sausage gravy. Make your own or do what I do—buy a cup-to-go from the Blanco Bowling Club and Cafe.

This requires a bread machine with a dough cycle. The recipe easily divides in half.

French Bread

1⅓ cups warm water
4 cups flour
2 teaspoons salt
3 teaspoons yeast

Place ingredients in bread machine according to manufacturer's directions (my faithful Hitachi requires the liquid first). Run the dough cycle; when done, remove dough. Shape into two long loaves, place on baking sheet or stone. Spray with water, allow to rest 20 to 40 minutes. Spray with water again. Bake at 400 degrees for 20 to 25 minutes.

Terry insisted that I include this cherished family recipe. His mother, Alice Naiser Rodgers, and her mother, Cecilia Goerig Naiser, made these Czech pigs-in-the-blanket the old-fashioned way—by kneading the dough. Alice later figured out an easier way—use a bread machine!

Klobasneakies

(phonetic spelling)
1 1-pound link sausage or 8 Polish link sausages
1⅓ cups milk
2½ tablespoons butter
2 eggs
1 tablespoon sugar
⅔ teaspoon salt
4 cups flour
2½ teaspoons yeast

Cut sausages into 48 pieces. Place remaining ingredients in bread machine, according to manufacturer's directions. Run the dough cycle. When done, remove dough. Cut into four equal portions. Cut one portion into 12 equal pieces. Shape one piece completely around one sausage piece and pinch dough to seal. Place on greased baking sheet. Do the same with the remaining dough and sausage pieces. Cover with a light towel or cloth napkin; allow to rise 30 minutes to an hour. Bake at 325 degrees until golden brown, about 20 minutes. Makes 4 dozen rolls. [Warning: these do NOT last long. Hide a few if you want some for yourself.]

Rosemary Rolls

1 cup plus 2 tablespoons water
2 tablespoons olive oil
2 tablespoons nonfat dry milk
½ cup instant potato flakes or buds
1 tablespoon sugar
1 teaspoon dry rosemary, crushed (fresh is better; snip in small pieces)

1 teaspoon salt
3 cups bread flour
1½ teaspoons dry yeast

Place ingredients in bread machine, according to manufacturer's instructions. Process on dough cycle. Remove dough; knead in additional flour if necessary to make dough easier to handle. Divide dough into 12 pieces (I make my rolls smaller). Form into rolls. Place on greased baking sheet. Cover; let rise until doubled, about 45 minutes. Bake at 375 degrees for 15 to 20 minutes. Delicious!

This is another one of my specialties and always gets a lot of raves at the table. Terry, my hunter, provides the venison.

Chili Cheese Steaks

2 pounds round steak (or venison), cut 1-inch thick
3 tablespoons flour
2 teaspoons salt
2 teaspoons chili powder
¼ teaspoon pepper
¼ cup or less shortening (I don't use any)
2 cups chopped onion
1 16-ounce can whole tomatoes
shredded cheddar cheese

In a skillet, brown meat in shortening or a little oil and place in a 9x13-inch baking dish. Brown onions in same pan until tender and stir in remaining ingredients except cheese. Pour over meat. Cover with foil. Bake 2 hours at 350 degrees. Or bake longer at a lower temperature. Sprinkle grated cheese on top and bake 5 minutes longer. Serve with white rice. Serves 4 to 6.

■■■■■■■■■■■■■■■■■■■■■■

Sheryl's Top 10 Favorite Old-Time Restaurants

1.　Po-Po Family Restaurant, Welfare
2.　Frank's Spaghetti House, Corpus Christi
3.　Earl Abel's, San Antonio
4.　Blue Bonnet Cafe, Marble Falls

5. Blanco Bowling Club and Cafe, Blanco
6. Bluebonnet Cafe, Temple
7. Hotel Blessing Coffee Shop, Blessing
8. Stagecoach Inn, Salado
9. Paris Coffee Shop, Fort Worth
10. Big Texan Steak Ranch, Amarillo

Historical Markers

Elite Cafe, Waco
Burton Cafe, Burton
Stagecoach Inn, Salado
Green Pastures, Austin
Wunsche Bros. Cafe & Saloon, Spring

National Register of Historic Places

Golden Light Cafe, Amarillo
Inn at Brushy Creek, Round Rock
Wunsche Bros. Cafe & Saloon, Spring

Restaurant Cookbooks

Green Pastures Cookbook, Alicia Garcés
Matt Martinez's Culinary Frontier: A Real Texas Cookbook,
Matt Martinez Jr. and Steve Pate
The Royers' Round Top Cafe: A Relational Odyssey
Secrets of the Original Don's Seafood & Steakhouse
What's Cooking at the Blue Bonnet Cafe, Belinda Kemper
Wunsche Bros. Cafe Cookbook, Brenda Greene Mitchell

Sheryl's Hall of Fame

Texas restaurants more than 50 years old

Oldest restaurants

1728	Kuby's (originally Germany), Dallas
1860s	Stagecoach Inn, Salado
1882	Fossati's Delicatessen, Victoria
1891	Michel's Drug Store, Marble Falls
1900	Weesatche Cafe, Weesatche
1902	Wunsche Bros. Cafe & Saloon, Spring
1906	Blessing Hotel Coffee Shop, Blessing
1910	City Cafe, Elgin
1911	Gaido's Seafood Restaurant, Galveston
	Las Lomas Restaurant, Irving
1912	The Tavern, Austin
1917	Christie's Seafood & Steaks Restaurant, Houston
	Schilo's, San Antonio
1918	El Fenix Mexican Restaurant, Dallas
1921	O.S.T. Restaurant, Bandera
1922	Millar Cafe and Soda Fountain, Grand Prairie
1923	James Coney Island, Houston
	Palace Cafe, Falls City
	Pig Stand, Beaumont
	Sulak's Cafe, West
1926	Mexican Inn Cafe, Fort Worth
	Paris Coffee Shop, Fort Worth
1927	Neely's Sandwich Shop, Marshall
1928	Green Frog Restaurant, Jacksboro
	New Waskom Cafe, Waskom
1929	Blue Bonnet Cafe, Marble Falls
	Bon Ton Restaurant, La Grange
	Bakery Cafe, Aransas Pass
	Cisco's Restaurant & Bakery, Austin
	Felix Mexican Restaurant, Houston
	Frank's Restaurant, Schulenburg
	Grey Moss Inn, Helotes

	Prince's Hamburgers, Dallas
	Sarah's Cafe, Fort Stockton
1920s	Club Cafe, Jefferson
	Nederland Lunch Counter, Nederland
1930	Floral Heights Cafe, Witchita Falls
	Quality Cafe, Beaumont
1931	Arlington Steak House, Arlington
	Dixie Pig Restaurant, Abilene
1932	La Fonda, San Antonio
1933	Keno's Cafe, Weslaco
1934	South Main Cafe (now South Main Depot Restaurant), Paris
	The Hoffbrau, Austin
1935	Joe T. Garcia's, Fort Worth
	Restaurant at Indian Lodge (now Black Bear Restaurant), Fort Davis
1936	Barth's Restaurant, Kenedy
	Cafe Texan, Huntsville
	Juicy Pig Cafe, Sherman
1937	Burton Cafe, Burton
	Caro's Restaurant, Rio Grande City
1938	Krause's Cafe, New Braunfels
	Mecca Restaurant, Dallas
	Po-Po Family Restaurant, Welfare
1939	Hung Fong Chinese Restaurant, San Antonio
	Hut's Hamburgers, Austin
	Town Cafe, Centerville
1930s	Club Cafe, Brady
	Doll House Cafe, Lubbock
	Santa Fe & SP Cafe, Brenham
1941	Elite Cafe, Waco
	Mi Tierra Cafe and Bakery, San Antonio
1943	Garza Cafe, San Juan
1944	Massa's Restaurant, Houston
	Sonny's Place, Galveston
1945	Elmer's Family Restaurant, El Paso
	King's Inn, Riviera

	New Braunfels Smokehouse Restaurant, New Braunfels
	Tom and Jo's Cafe, Denton
1946	Casa Rio, San Antonio
	Duck Inn, Rockport
	Golden Light Cafe, Amarillo
	Green Pastures Restaurant, Austin
	Hermann Sons Steak House, Hondo
	Shorty's Place, Falls City
1947	Blanco Bowling Club and Cafe, Blanco
	Campisi's Egyptian, Dallas
	Cattlemen's Fort Worth Steak House, Fort Worth
	Dairy Queen, Austin
	Frank's Spaghetti House, Corpus Christi
	Malt House, San Antonio
	Round Top Cafe, Round Top
1948	Big State Drug's Fountain & Grill, Irving
	Bluebonnet Cafe, Temple
	Jake and Dorothy's Cafe, Stephenville
	Ranchman's Cafe, Ponder
1949	Health Camp, Waco
	Jacala Mexican Restaurant, San Antonio
	Johnny Cace Seafood & Steak House, Longview
	Loggins Restaurant, Tyler
1940s	El Ranchito, Seguin
	Star Cafe, Fort Worth
1950	Fuller's Fine Food, Tyler
	Goodson's Cafe, Tomball
	Texas Grill, Ballinger
	Whataburger, Corpus Christi

Recipe Index

Main Entrees

Desserts

Other stuff

Restaurant Index (Alphabetical Listing)